D1633879

John Osborne's

Look Back in Anger

Continuum Modern Theatre Guides

Aleks Sierz

John Osborne's
Look Back in Anger

continuum

Continuum

The Tower Building, 11 York Road, London SE1 7NX

80 Maiden Lane, Suite 704, New York NY 10038

www.continuumbooks.com

First published 2008

British Library Cataloguing-in-Publication Data
A catalogue record for this book is available from the British Library.

ISBN: 978-0-8264-9202-9 (hardback)
          978-0-8264-9201-2 (paperback)

Library of Congress Cataloging-in-Publication Data
A catalog record for this book is available from the Library of Congress.

Typeset by Kenneth Burnley, Wirral, Cheshire
Printed and bound in Great Britain by MPG Books Ltd, Bodmin, Cornwall

Contents

General Preface

Continuum Modern Theatre Guides

Volumes in the series Continuum Modern Theatre Guides offer concise and informed introductions to the key plays of modern times. Each book takes a close look at one particular play's dramaturgical qualities and then at its various theatrical manifestations. The books are carefully structured to offer a systematic study of the play in its biographical, historical, social and political context, followed by an in-depth study of the text and a chapter which outlines the work's production history, examining both the original productions of the play and subsequent major stage interpretations. Where relevant, screen adaptations will also be analyzed. There then follows a chapter dedicated to workshopping the play, based on suggested group exercises. Also included are a timeline and suggestions for further reading.

Each book covers:

- Background and context
- Analysis of the play
- Production history
- Workshopping exercises

The aim is to provide accessible introductions to modern plays for students in both Theatre/Performance Studies and English, as well as for informed general readers. The series includes up-to-date coverage of a broad range of key plays, with summaries of important critical approaches and the intellectual debates that have illuminated the meaning of the work and made a significant contribution to our broader cultural life. They will enable readers to develop their understanding of playwrights and theatre-makers, as well as inspiring them to broaden their studies.

The Editors:
Steve Barfield, Janelle Reinelt,
Graham Saunders and Aleks Sierz

March 2008

Acknowledgements

I would firstly like to thank my fellow series editors, who have offered intellectual, practical and moral support throughout: Steve Barfield, Janelle Reinelt and Graham Saunders. Although I have not quoted at length from the interviews that I conducted as research for the book, the interviewees were all extremely helpful: Richard Baron, Richard Coyle, Emma Fielding, Peter Gill, Jacqueline Glasser, Scott Graham, David Hare, Gregory Hersov, Steve Hoggett, Marcus Romer, Michael Sheen, Derek Smith, David Tennant, Wendy Williams. Thanks for all your help.

The workshop chapter owes everything to a memorable week-long workshop with third-year acting students at Rose Bruford College, Sidcup, held in February 2007. So my sincerest regards to Robert Amundsen, Adrian Decosta, Teddy Goddard, Jessica Gunning, Shonel Jackson, Simone James, Lena Kaur, Martin Winsley, Kelly Wood and Tonin Zefi. Thanks guys, you really rock. I'd also like to thank the staff at Rose Bruford College for helping make this event a success, and especially Nesta Jones, Pat O'Toole and David Zoob.

I would also like to thank Alexis Amey (Public Eye), Beckah Cross (Royal Court), Alexa DeGennaro (Boston University), Gordon Dickerson, John Goodfellow (Royal Exchange, Manchester), Joe Hill-Gibbins, Helen Iball (Hull), Stephen Lacey (Glamorgan), Peter Leone, Mary Luckhurst (York), Katy Mckay (Harrowgate), Kate Morley (Blueprint), Heather Neill, Stephen Pidcock (Royal Court), Dan Rebellato (Royal Holloway), Harriet Robinson, Al Senter, Dominic Shellard (Sheffield), Robert

Tanitch, Becky Thomas (Faber), Ewan Thompson (Royal Court), Anna Tune (ICM), Peter Whitebrook, Agata Witczak (Lodz) and Dinah Wood (Faber).

The staff at the embattled Theatre Museum were both knowledgeable and helpful. I'd also like to thank the participants in the following events, which marked the fiftieth anniversary of *Look Back in Anger*: 'Oh Mr and Mrs Porter!', Theatre Museum, London, 19 March 2006; 'John Heilpern in Conversation with Michael Billington', Royal Court, London, 4 May 2006; 'Look Back in Anger: A Tribute', Royal Court, 8 May 2006; '1956, 1968, 1979, 1995: New Historiographies of Post-War British Theatre', conference at Royal Holloway, University of London, 11–13 May 2006; 'More Than Just Osborne', British Library, 5 September 2006. In different ways, you all helped.

And my publisher, Anna Sandeman, along with the rest of the staff at Continuum, namely Colleen Coalter and Anya Wilson, were knowledgeable, efficient and helpful.

All quotations from John Osborne's *Look Back in Anger* appear with kind permission from Faber and Faber Ltd. For the USA, permission has been granted by The Arvon Foundation. Permission to perform the play in the USA should be made in writing prior to the commencement of rehearsals to Gordon Dickerson, 2 Crescent Grove, London SW4 7AH, UK.

And, as always, my heartfelt thanks for inspiration and encouragement to Lia Ghilardi.

ALEKS SIERZ
London, July 2007

1 Background and Context

This chapter is an introduction to the study of John Osborne's *Look Back in Anger*. It explains why the play is important, gives a sketch of its author's life and discusses the social, economic and political background to the play.

Introduction

Look Back in Anger is the most famous new play of post-war British theatre – its significance, quite simply, is that it changed the history of theatre. It is one of the few works of drama that are indisputably central to British life, and its name is one of the most evocative in cultural history. Its opening night, on 8 May 1956, rapidly became legendary as 'the event which marks "then" off decisively from "now"' – no less than a 'revolution' (Taylor, 1969: 9, 14, 28). *Look Back in Anger* was important because it sparked off the first New Wave of what came to be known as Kitchen-Sink Drama: it expressed the sensibility of the Angry Young Men and Jimmy Porter, its anti-hero, became the spokesman of a whole generation. Osborne's play is a key milestone in new writing for British theatre, and the Royal Court theatre – which produced the play – has since become the country's most important new writing venue. In 1999, the play was voted one of the top five 'most significant plays of the century' in NT 2000, a National Theatre poll. And it remains highly relevant: Osborne 'made the future possible,' writes *Guardian* theatre critic Michael Billington; 'You can draw a line through post-war British drama linking Look Back in Anger with

Shopping and Fucking' (Billington, 1999). Moreover, in one of the many articles that appeared to mark the play's 50th anniversary, one cultural commentator wrote: 'The legend is that Look Back in Anger changed British theatre for ever, replacing stage-sets of Belgravia mansions with a drab Midlands flat, and smart upper-class remarks with the angry anti-establishment rants of its hero, Jimmy Porter' (Lawson, 2006).

Despite its legendary aura, *Look Back in Anger* is essentially a domestic drama about a married couple, Jimmy and Alison, who share their Midlands flat with Cliff, Jimmy's friend. Despite its domesticity, it has proved to be an icon factory: firstly, it was the crucible in which the myth of the Angry Young Men was forged. George Fearon, the Royal Court's press officer, disliked the play and scornfully said to Osborne: 'I suppose you're really – an angry young man' (Osborne, 1991: 20). As the play gradually made its mark, the Angry Young Man label was taken up by newspapers, radio and television, creating the first post-war media frenzy in culture. The result was a cultural movement that was fabricated out of a group of diverse talents, such as novelists Kingsley Amis, John Wain, John Braine, Alan Sillitoe and philosopher Colin Wilson. None of them were happy to be called Angry Young Men, and the fullest study of the phenomenon concludes that, despite its cultural impact, 'the entire notion of the grouping was entirely unjustified' (Ritchie, 1988: 207). Secondly, the play's comparatively squalid set suggested the idea of Kitchen-Sink Drama, despite the fact that no such domestic necessity was visible on the original set. And, by the late 1950s, Kitchen-Sink Drama had become an established theatrical genre. Lastly, the relationship between the play's main characters, Jimmy and Alison, has been turned into readily identifiable symbols: the cover of the current playtext shows an ironing board with a red tie draped over it. The ironing board conveys a sense of traditional domestic drudgery while the tie is a phallic symbol, its colour signifying anger with a hint of left-wing radicalism.

As well as producing such icons, *Look Back in Anger* is itself a powerful symbol of post-war British theatre. It not only revolutionized a staid, stuffy and outdated theatre culture, introducing an urgent contemporary voice, but it also became the foundation myth of the Royal Court theatre and British new writing in general. If this play hadn't existed, the history of post-war British drama would have looked very different. Most playwrights of the late 1950s to the 1970s – such as Arnold Wesker, Tom Stoppard, David Hare and David Edgar – acknowledge the importance and inspiration of *Look Back in Anger*. In 1958, Harold Pinter played Cliff at the Intimate theatre, Palmer's Green, north London. *Look Back in Anger*'s centrality is a foundation myth, but a foundation myth with strong support from the theatre community. As Edgar says, 'Surely no British play of the twentieth century can have so assuredly and rapidly taken its times by the throat' (Edgar, 1988: 137). And Hare insists: 'John [Osborne] *did* transform the British theatre in 1956, everything *was* different afterwards, he *is* the gate-keeper. [. . .] It's a fact: he changed the British theatre' (Palmer, 2006). Although it was not an overnight success, *Look Back in Anger* has been constantly revived. In 1993, Osborne boasted that 'somewhere in the world the play is performed every night' (Osborne, 1996b: xiii).

The influence of *Look Back in Anger* and the Angry Young Men permeated British culture in thousands of ways. Some of these are well known; others more obscure. For example, before it was made into a film starring Cliff Richard, *Expresso Bongo* (1958) was a stage show nicknamed 'The Angry Young Musical' (Fowler, 2005: 67) while a recent play, Bridget O'Donnell's *Lie Back in Anger* (2006), made an obvious reference to the original. In the wider popular culture, 'Me used to be Angry Young Man' is a line from the Beatles' song 'Getting Better' on the legendary *Sgt Pepper's Lonely Hearts Club Band* album (1967), 'Look Back in Anger' is a song on David Bowie's 1979 album *Lodger* and 'Don't Look Back in Anger'

is on the 1995 Oasis album *(What's the Story) Morning Glory?*
There have been jokes about a library strike (Book Lack in Ongar),
Angry Young Men are continually being spotted somewhere and
'John Osbore' was a running joke during the 1960s in the satirical
magazine *Private Eye*. If the 1950s were immediately labelled *The
Angry Decade*, in Kenneth Allsop's 1958 book of that name, a more
recent work, *The Angry Island* by A. A. Gill, argues that anger is a
national characteristic: 'Collectively and individually, the English
are angry' (Gill, 2005: 7). In 2007, when *Celebrity Big Brother*
contestant Jade Goody was evicted from the show, her hometown
wasn't keen on seeing her, hence the headline 'Look back in
Ongar'; and a review of an Asian play in the *Times Literary Supple-
ment* gave us 'Look back in bhangra'. Even today, the play's title
remains a legend: a Google search yields more than a million web
pages.

   Look Back in Anger is not just an old play, it's a cultural battle-
field. Few works continue to arouse such strong emotions. 'If you
express any scepticism about the conventional story you wind up
being called a "revisionist", as if questioning the play's axiomatic
significance to our theatre has a whiff of Holocaust-denial about it'
(Rebellato, 2006: 527–8). Because of its immense impact, *Look
Back in Anger* has inevitably attracted criticism as well as praise.
It has been condemned for being conservative in form, dutifully
naturalistic rather than experimental and imaginatively theatrical –
by contrast, Samuel Beckett's *Waiting for Godot* (1955) has been
lauded as the really revolutionary text of the mid-1950s (Shellard,
1999: 46–7, 69–71). True, perhaps, but it's worth remembering
that *Look Back in Anger* quickly became a repertory favourite
nationwide (Fowler, 2005: 46), unlike *Waiting for Godot*, which
remained a metropolitan phenomenon. Compared to Beckett's
play, *Look Back in Anger* also represented the revenge of English
naturalism on European experimentalism. One cultural historian
states that 'Most theatre historians now agree that *Look Back in*

Anger was not really a revolution at all' (Sandbrook, 2006: 193). If only things were that simple. The truth is that the play remains a contested territory, and while people still care about theatre history, the skirmishes will rumble on.

Admittedly, the plotting of Osborne's play is clunky: its characters spend much of their time telling the audience their life stories, and Helena's exit at the end is an unrealistic device to bring Jimmy and Alison back together again. Indeed, in common with many other debut plays, the author has a lot to say but can't quite find the right form to say it in. So *Look Back in Anger* remains stubbornly of its time, resisting all attempts to update it. Nor has the charismatic Jimmy escaped criticism. Although successive generations have found ready answers to the carping question 'What is he angry about?', they have been less forgiving of Osborne for making Jimmy a mouthpiece for his own prejudices. In particular, his attitude to women and gays has been robustly criticized. Jimmy has even been denounced for being a wife-beater, despite the fact that there is no evidence of this in the text. Nowadays, a play such as Shelagh Delaney's *A Taste of Honey* (1958) is seen as a much more sympathetic view of sexuality, and of race. In today's climate, it is even possible to see *Look Back in Anger*'s most original contribution to 1950s cultural sensibility – its expression of masculine feelings – as just part of confessional culture. What was rare in the 1950s – men talking about emotions – is now general. Still, the play's relevance stubbornly persists. For example, the magisterial *Cambridge History of British Theatre* concludes, 'It was a contemporary British play dealing with contemporary British themes. However much later critics might wish to qualify the relevance of those themes, to deny the impact is to ignore the weight of historical evidence" (Bull, 2004: 336).

Bearing in mind the often mean-spirited attacks on *Look Back in Anger*, perhaps it is time to rescue the play from the enormous condescension of posterity and acknowledge once again its historic importance and its continued contemporary relevance. Above all, it still tells us who we are: 'Fifty years later and *Look Back in Anger* still means something central to our theatre, our culture, even ourselves' (Rebellato, 2006: 529). On stage, its spirit of attack and combative air is still thrilling; Osborne's voice remains compellingly articulate, instantly recognizable and theatrically exciting. His challenge to conventional wisdom and cant is still inspiring; his examination of emotional aggression and personal timidity is still relevant. Whatever you think of the play, Osborne's position as the one playwright who started a revolution in post-war British theatre is hard to deny. But as well as being culturally significant, *Look Back in Anger* is of interest in itself. Despite its flaws, it is a complex play that works brilliantly on stage, burning itself into your memory and leaving you with the sense of having witnessed the true emotions of real human beings, in their attractive ugliness as well as their terrible beauty.

About the play's author

In *Look Back in Anger*, Jimmy has a key speech in which he says: 'I knew more about – love . . . betrayal . . . and death, when I was ten years old than you will probably ever know all your life' (59). But how autobiographical is the play? John James Osborne was born in rented rooms in Fulham, London, on 12 December 1929. His father, Thomas, worked as an advertising copywriter in Fleet Street until his health collapsed due to tuberculosis; his mother, Nellie Beatrice, was a barmaid. It is usually unwise to use biography to explain a writer's work, but it is surely significant that the surname of Osborne's cousin was Porter, and that, when John was aged ten, his father died. About five years later, John was expelled from Belmont, his boarding school in Devon, for hitting the headmaster, and he began working as a cub reporter for *The Gas World*, a trade newspaper. He soon left to join a touring repertory theatre company as an assistant stage manager, and then worked, not very successfully, as an actor, mainly outside London. To make ends meet, he often had to deliver the Christmas post. While working as an actor, he tried his hand at writing.

Although *Look Back in Anger* is seen as Osborne's debut, it was not his first play. In 1949, he wrote *The Devil Inside Him*, in collaboration with actress Stella Linden, his lover, and this had a brief run at the Theatre Royal, Huddersfield, in 1950. He then teamed up with Anthony Creighton, another actor, in an unsuccessful and barely legal repertory company, Saga, in Ilfracombe. After this, on 23 June 1951, Osborne married actress Pamela Lane at Bridgwater in Somerset. Although the couple were often separated by the conflicting demands of work, they shared a Hammersmith flat with Creighton for a while. In 1955, *Personal Enemy* – co-written by the two men – was staged at Harrogate, and they also co-wrote *Epitaph for George Dillon*, although that wasn't staged until 1957, following the success of *Look Back in Anger*. After Osborne's death, Creighton claimed to have had a homosexual affair with him, but there is no evidence that Osborne was anything but straight. He kept writing and penned *Look Back in Anger* about a year after his first marriage broke up in 1954. His pocket diary records that, on 4 May 1955, he 'began writing' and that, on 3 June, '*Look Back in Anger* finished' (Osborne, 1981: 264–6). He then spent a couple of weeks typing up copies. As the original manuscript of the play shows, Osborne wrote in a passion, leaving it almost unrevised and unchanged. He didn't do rewrites. The speed of composition is evident not only in the rapid shifts of thought in Jimmy's speeches but also in their uncensored directness. Given the play's evocative title, it is interesting to note that Osborne considered six alternatives – including *Man in a Rage*, *Close the Cage Behind You* and *My Blood Is a Mile High* – before choosing *Look Back in Anger*, which had, incidentally, been the title of the Christian socialist Leslie Paul's 1951 autobiography.

Osborne sent *Look Back in Anger* to the main agents and theatre managements and it was turned down by all of them. By then, this outsider was living with Creighton on a barge on the river Thames. Looking through *The Stage*, the actors' newspaper, Osborne saw an advert by the English Stage Company asking for plays. This new company, led by artistic director George Devine, had recently taken over the Royal Court theatre with a mission to revive British drama. But good new work was hard to find: of the 750 plays submitted in response to its advert, only *Look Back in Anger* was chosen for a production. It was the third play in an opening season which included novelist Angus Wilson's *The Mulberry Bush*, American playwright Arthur Miller's *The Crucible*, versifier Ronald Duncan's *Don Juan* and *The Death of Satan*, and novelist Nigel Dennis's *Cards of Identity*. The theatre also hosted the British debut of German director Bertolt Brecht's Berliner Ensemble. But new plays did badly at the box office and the theatre was saved financially by a Christmas revival of William Wycherley's Restoration comedy, *The Country Wife*. Devine, aged 44, first met Osborne in August 1955, when he rowed to Osborne and Creighton's barge from his eighteenth-century house next to Hammersmith Bridge. On the way he capsized, but borrowed a dingy to complete the journey. After talking to Osborne, he offered the playwright £25 to produce the play, as well as employing him as an assistant stage manager, actor and play reader. Tony Richardson, Devine's 25-year-old associate, was keen on the play and directed its first production. He recalled in his autobiography that 'rehearsals were terse and a bit glum' (Richardson, 1993: 78). Osborne's phrase was 'subdued and unspeculative' (Osborne, 1991: 18). One day, Richardson said that the third act was sagging and suggested a song: Osborne wrote the Flanagan and Allen parody (85–6) while going home on the bus.

Look Back in Anger took a while to become a success, but Osborne was soon in demand. His follow-up, *The Entertainer*

(Royal Court, 1957), drew parallels between the failure of Archie Rice, a shabby music-hall comedian, and the decline of the British Empire. Against the background of the Suez Crisis, the play – which starred a dazzling Laurence Olivier – mixed music-hall routines (much loved by its author) and straight drama. After being hyped as an Angry Young Man, Osborne lived up to the part, writing provocative articles excoriating the complacency of British society. Pieces such as 'They Call It Cricket' and 'A Letter to My Fellow Countrymen' are a joy to read. Despite the failure of his next musical play, *The World of Paul Slickey* (Palace Theatre, 1959), an unusual satire on journalism, Osborne had another great success with *Luther* (Royal Court, 1961). Here, the German Protestant reformer, Martin Luther, was embodied in a mesmerizing performance by the young Albert Finney. This was followed by another failure, the insubstantial *Plays for England* (Royal Court, 1962), as well as other successes such as the Oscar-winning screenplay of *Tom Jones* (1963) and the play *Inadmissible Evidence* (Royal Court, 1964). The latter, starring Nicol Williamson as the lawyer Bill Maitland, was a sheering portrait of a man whose life was disintegrating. In 1965, Osborne's *A Patriot for Me* returned to a historical theme, the case of the Austrian Colonel Alfred Redl. Banned by the Lord Chamberlain, the theatre censor, for its depiction of a drag ball, the play was nevertheless staged by the Royal Court in a club performance, a way of evading censorship. During the last week of the production, George Devine – who was playing the Baron – collapsed from a heart attack, and he died in 1966.

In 1968, the Royal Court staged Osborne's *Time Present* and *A Hotel in Amsterdam* (with Paul Scofield), in which he satirized the permissive society. This led to a backlash and complaints that the Angry Young Man had become a middle-aged reactionary. His next plays – *West of Suez* (Royal Court, 1971), *A Sense of Detachment* (Royal Court, 1972), *The End of Me Old Cigar* (Greenwich, 1975) and *Watch It Come Down* (National, 1976) – showed him abandoning his original sense of theatrical form and writing opinionated squibs for increasingly uninterested audiences. Osborne also adapted plays by authors such as Lope de Vega, William Shakespeare and Henrik Ibsen, and wrote plays for television, such as *A Subject of Scandal and Concern* (1960) and *The Gift of Friendship* (1974). He also wrote a highly readable two-volume autobiography, *A Better Class of Person* (1981) and *Almost a Gentleman* (1991). In 1992, he returned to theatre with the much-scorned *Déjà vu* (Comedy Theatre), a play which revisits *Look Back in Anger* 35 years on, starring aged characters called J. P. (Jimmy Porter) and Cliff, with Alison being J. P.'s daughter.

In the late 1950s, Osborne was labelled a left-wing playwright, partly because he played up to the image of the Angry Young Man and partly because he did occasionally support causes such as the Ban the Bomb marches. For this reason, he is often seen as having drifted towards the right, becoming a Grumpy Old Man. In truth, he was always more of a passionate individualist than a joiner of any causes, and his anger was directed at the unfeeling complacency of modern life. His official biographer describes him as a contradictory genius, part depressive, part romantic, part defiant patriot: 'a Cavalier *and* a Roundhead, a traditionalist in revolt, a radical who hated change, a protector of certain musty old English values, a born dissenter who wasn't *nice*' (Heilpern, 2006: 15). In *Almost a Gentleman*, for example, Osborne makes the typically provocative statement: 'Whatever else, I have been blessed with God's two greatest gifts: to be born English and heterosexual' (Osborne, 1991: 272). Photographs reveal a gradual change from impoverished actor to ban-the-bomb protester, and from stylish 1960s teddy boy to tweed-coated country gent.

Osborne's personal life was deeply marked by the loss of his father and his love–hate relationship with his mother. He was married four times: in 1957, to Mary Ure, the actress who created the role of Alison; in 1963 to critic Penelope Gilliatt; in 1968 to actress Jill Bennett; and in 1978 to critic Helen Dawson. He valued loyalty above all else and was unforgiving when crossed: after a quarrel, he abandoned his daughter Nolan when she was 17.

Osborne died in Shropshire on Christmas Eve 1994, from complications after he had developed diabetes. Earlier in the same year, he published a typically acerbic collection of his prose, entitled *Damn You, England*.

The social, economic and political context

Look Back in Anger doesn't mention any contemporary political events, but it is full of references to the mid-1950s political, social and cultural zeitgeist. The broadest backdrop to the play is the rise and fall of the British Empire. From its slow beginnings in the early seventeenth century, the British Empire grew enormously until, by the death of Queen Victoria in 1901, it was the largest empire ever known. The proud boast was that the sun never set on the quarter of the world's land area and fifth of its population governed by Britain. The zenith of Empire did not last long, however. The lifespan of an individual such as Winston Churchill (1874–1965) covers its final rise and fall. After the end of the Second World War in 1945, former colonies rapidly achieved independence, most notably India in 1947. In Osborne's play, Colonel Redfern – Alison's father – sketches out his own career as an imperial administrator in India: 'It was March, 1914, when I left England, and, apart from leaves every ten years or so, I didn't see much of my own country until we all came back in '47.' His job was to command 'the Maharajah's army', a reminder that Britain relied on co-opted local rulers in order to maintain imperial control. The Colonel looks back with a mixture of pride and resentment: 'I think the last day the sun shone was when that dirty little train steamed out of that crowded, suffocating Indian station, and the battalion band playing for all it was worth' (70). And Jimmy says, 'The old Edwardian brigade do make their brief little world look pretty tempting' (11). The notion of Empire was familiar to all who saw the play in 1956, less than a decade after Indian independence. In *Observer* critic Kenneth Tynan's review of the original production, he expands on Jimmy's character: 'One cannot imagine Jimmy Porter listening with a straight face to speeches about our inalienable right to flog Cypriot schoolboys' (Tynan, 2007: 113). Until 1960, Cyprus was still governed by Britain, and corporal punishment remained common in British institutions throughout the 1960s.

Although *Look Back in Anger* alludes briefly to the Second World War, Jimmy is more concerned with its precursor in European power politics, the Spanish Civil War. His father, he says, came back 'from the war in Spain. And certain God-fearing gentlemen there had made such a mess of him, he didn't have long left to live' (58). Like many young men who joined the anti-fascist International Brigade, Jimmy's father fought on the losing side in the Spanish Civil War. This conflict between the ruling left-wing Republicans (supported by communists, socialists and anarchists) and the rebel right-wing Nationalists (supported by business, church and army) in 1936–9 was won by General Francisco Franco's nationalist armies, supported by the fascist dictators Hitler and Mussolini, and many saw it as a dress rehearsal for world war. One of the many results of the Second World War, the loss of Britain's imperial role and the rise of American global power, is also alluded to by numerous references in the text. At one point, Jimmy jokes about living in 'the American age' (11). At another, the idea of having 'some poor British actor' play a part in a Hollywood film reflects a feeling of British cultural inferiority (16). There was also a dark side to this brave new post-war world: the Cold War and the abundance of nuclear weapons. In May 1956, a civil-defence exercise took place in London and Birmingham, based on the hypothesis that 10-megaton hydrogen bombs had been dropped. Nuclear annihilation was a real fear.

While the loss of Empire forms the broad background of *Look Back in Anger*, Britain's international role also affected the way in which it was understood. Although it premiered in May 1956, it was events in the autumn of that year – when the play was broadcast on television – that gave it wider political resonance. Since 1883, British troops had protected the Suez Canal – an essential sea route to India – as part of British Imperial control of Egypt. On 26 July 1956, Colonel Gamal Abdel Nasser – the leader of Egypt, which had been independent since 1922 – nationalized the canal. When Nasser rejected an ultimatum, British, French and Israeli forces attacked Egypt in October. The Suez Crisis proved disastrous: British public opinion was outraged by Prime Minister Anthony Eden's decision to use force, and the United States, irritated at not being consulted, forced him to climb down. The events of 1956 were an international humiliation for Britain because they proved that the country was no longer a world power. This realization gave *Look Back in Anger* a resonance it did not originally have.

Look Back in Anger's Jimmy, as the reviews of its first production show, was seen in a surprisingly consistent way as a spokesman for his generation. Jimmy was a symbol of youth discontented with the status quo. Like so many young people in the 1950s, he benefited from the 1944 Education Act (the Butler Act, named after Conservative education minister R. A. Butler), which made it easier for people of modest backgrounds to go to university. Unlike most members of the Establishment, such as Alison's brother Nigel and his friends, Jimmy has not been to public school or Oxbridge. He's been to a newer university, which he jokingly calls 'white tile' rather than redbrick (41). Tynan's review of the play opened with a line alluding to this: '"They are scum" was Mr [Somerset] Maugham's famous verdict on the class of State-aided university students', before proudly calling the play 'all scum and a mile wide' (Tynan, 2007: 112). Significantly enough, Nigel has been to Sandhurst, a military college and symbol of conservative England. Jimmy opposes the whole conservative Establishment: he mocks class distinctions, public schools, politicians, bishops, and the nuclear deterrent. For him, the torpor of a normal English Sunday afternoon sums up the nation's lethargy, and he despises anything 'posh' or 'phoney', such as the trendy admiration of French culture.

In the 1950s, the idea of revolution was close to people's consciousness. The Russian Revolution had happened as recently as 1917, and the Soviet dictator Stalin had been an ally in the Second World War. At one point, Jimmy says, 'If the revolution ever comes, I'll be the first to be put up against the wall' (34). But the British left, which had supported the Republican side in the Spanish Civil War, was experiencing profound changes. In April 1956, Nikita Krushchev, the new Soviet leader, denounced Stalin to a meeting of the Communist Party Congress, admitting the injustice of Stalinist oppression. This caused a crisis among Britain's left-wing intellectuals, and – combined with events in Hungary when the Soviet army quelled a popular uprising in November 1956 – led to some 7,000 members (almost a fifth of the total) resigning from the British Communist Party. Out of the turmoil, the New Left – which was equally critical of Soviet dictatorship, liberal democracy and capitalism – was formed, drawing its strength mainly from intellectuals and students. Figures such as E. P. Thompson, Stuart Hall, Raymond Williams and Ralph Milliband rejected both Communist Party and Labour Party, while advocating a more libertarian and radical form of socialism. Although their main arena of activity was in education and publishing, they influenced the climate of dissident thought. Direct action was expressed through the Campaign for Nuclear Disarmament, which by 1961 could mobilize 100,000 protesters to march on Trafalgar Square. The Royal Court banner could be seen on CND's annual Aldermaston march as New Wave met New Left. Although some on the New Left criticized *Look Back in Anger* for its lack of a political programme, other intellectuals co-opted Jimmy to the cause. Tynan, for example, writing in a liberal Sunday news-paper, saw in the play 'an instinctive leftishness' (Tynan, 2007: 113).

But 1956 also marked a moment of transition from one kind of culture to another: 'The year is a highly visible moment within a longer process of cultural change that sees the UK adjusting to social democracy, to a post-imperial reality of subordination to US interests, to an unprecedented affluence driven by consumerism, which in turn produced a transformation of culture' (Lacey, 2006: 3). One area where this change could be seen was the rise of youth culture. By the mid-1950s, the teenager had been invented both as a target of the consumer society and as the object of outrage. Teenagers were a huge new market for clothes, music, radios and other goods; they were also seen as frighteningly violent, sexually promiscuous and distressingly bad-mannered. 'Youth' became a vital repository of society's fears: the Welfare State and the Age of Affluence had created the Generation Gap and moral panics about ungrateful, angry youth. Deviancy was born, and pop culture. The year 1956 was the date of Lonnie Donegan's hit 'Rock Island Line', Elvis Presley's first album for Sun records, the film *Rock Around the Clock*, and teddy boys slashing cinema seats. A Royal Court flyer for *Look Back in Anger* originally described Jimmy as an English 'Rebel without a Cause', a reference to the iconic James Dean film of 1955 (Fowler, 2005: 39). For the older generation, the fear of youth was applied indiscriminately to teddy boys and university leftists alike. Of course, Jimmy is not a typical teenager: he's too old, and he's too snobbish. He calls working-class lads 'yobs' (8), and instead of rock 'n' roll, he prefers jazz, a much more intellectu-ally respectable music, popular with students. But he was certainly seen as a spokesman of the new generation, and Tynan – in his typically myth-making mode – claimed that '*Look Back in Anger* is likely to remain a minority taste. What matters, however, is the size of the minority. I estimate it at roughly 6,733,000, which is the number of people in this country between the ages of twenty and thirty' (Tynan, 2007: 113). Clearly, this included the university types and supporters of the New Left who were interested in theatre, itself an endangered art form. By 1952, a third of Victorian theatres had been converted into cinemas; between 1950 and 1955, the number of repertory theatres almost halved.

As is clear from Jimmy's tastes, *Look Back in Anger* is at a cultural crossroads. He's deeply engaged with traditional notions of Englishness, especially with the way that national character is expressed in literature. Like a true patriot, Jimmy alludes to poems such as Rudyard Kipling's 'The White Man's Burden' and T. S. Eliot's *The Waste Land*, even when he's provoking his wife. Jimmy gently mocks such quintessentially English figures as the poet William Wordsworth and writer J. B. Priestley, and yet he likes the music of Vaughan Williams. He also quotes Shakespeare and the Romantic poets. But Englishness is for him a masculine heterosexual culture – when he talks about homosexuals, he uses foreign references, French novelist André Gide, Italian artist Michelangelo Buonarroti or Greek Chorus Boys. But his references to mass culture – American game shows (*The Sixty-Four Dollar Question*) and Hollywood films (Marlon Brando) – are a reminder of the culture wars of the 1950s, in which a generation of influential British critics, led by Richard Hoggart and Raymond Williams, criticized the soporific effects of mass culture. Hoggart's *The Uses of Literacy* (1957) showed a 'concern for cultural, rather than political values' (Hewison, 1988: 217) and Williams's *Culture and Society* (1958), influenced by F. R. Leavis, 'was the key book' (Sinfield, 1989: 241) because it argued, from a left-wing perspective, that high culture and middle-class dissidence were essential to preserving traditional community values in the face of American popular culture. In this context, 1956 was also significant as the first full year in which a commercial television channel, ITV, directly challenged the hegemony of state broadcaster, the BBC.

Such attitudes were an example of the fact that, in Britain, so much energy went into discussing the politics of culture. As affluence increased, so did fears of a withering of the human spirit. And the place to combat that was culture. Thus the New Left placed the criticism of mass media 'at the centre of their thinking' (Rebellato, 1999: 32). Plainly, it was easier for the middle classes and for intellectuals to make radical breakthroughs in culture than in politics. In 1958, the radical Parisian magazine *Internationale Situationniste* argued that English culture was 30 years behind the times, and condemned the Angry Young Men as '*même particulièrement réactionnaires en ceci qu'ils attribuent une valuer privilégiée, un sens de rachat, à l'exercise de la littérature* [particularly reactionary in their attribution of a privileged, redemptive value to the practice of literature]' (5). Thus French radicals attacked the idea that culture could be as radical as politics (see Sierz, 1996).

The audience for 1950s new drama is usually characterized as young, lower-middle class and left-liberal. For this group, the working class was an object of fascination and the idea of anger as exemplified by Jimmy offered a radical identity which helped them cope with the insecurity of rapid social change (see Sinfield, 1989: 253, 260–1). It glamorized the politics of negativity and provided a role model. The popular image of *Look Back in Anger* and the cultural phenomenon of the Angry Young Man was that of a youthful rebellion. So it was the 'combination of events across the political and cultural spectrum that made the moment of 1956 such a powerful challenge to post-war consensus' (Lacey, 2006: 4). A variety of events – imperial, political, social and economic – combined to make 1956 an *annus mirabilis* (Hewison, 1988: 148). But what of the play itself?

2 Analysis and Commentary

This chapter is a study of *Look Back in Anger* both as a dramatic text and as a performed play that has excited comment and provoked analysis. Although plot summaries are often seen as old-fashioned, they are useful in sketching out the action of the play, before undertaking a broader analysis of its characters, influences, images, themes and key scenes.

Plot summary

Act One

Look Back in Anger is set in an attic flat in the Midlands during the mid-1950s. Jimmy Porter is about 25 years old and a lower-middle-class university graduate married to Alison, who comes from an upper-class family. The set is the one room they occupy, and they live with Cliff, a young Welshman who has his own (offstage) room. It's early evening in April, and the play opens with Jimmy and Cliff sitting and reading the Sunday newspapers, while Alison stands at the ironing board pressing their clothes. It soon emerges that Jimmy and Cliff make a living from running a sweet stall and that Jimmy resents the higher social status of his wife. Jimmy's monologues deride Britain as a nation slumbering in post-war inertia, and he goads both Alison and Cliff about their lethargy. Still, they remain affectionate, if sometimes exasperated. Typically, Jimmy '*bangs his breast theatrically*', and says, 'Why don't we have a little game? Let's pretend that we're human beings, and that we're actually alive' (9). But this attempt to provoke his flatmates is also laced with a nostalgia for the past: Jimmy is attracted by the ideal of long Edwardian summers when the sun never set on the British Empire: 'If you've no world of your own, it's rather pleasant to regret the passing of someone else's' (11). Jimmy's abusive tirades combine a hatred of Alison's family and an antagonism to women in general. During his fevered attempts to provoke the rather cool Alison into losing her temper, Cliff acts as a peacemaker between them. While Jimmy demands a reaction, Alison just wants some peace. The targets of Jimmy's ire include Alison's brother Nigel and her mother. At one point, things escalate when Cliff wrestles Jimmy to the ground to make him apologize 'for being nasty to everyone' (21). In the ensuing grapple, Jimmy pushes Cliff into the ironing board and Alison's arm gets burnt. Although Jimmy is sorry, Alison orders him out of the room.

Alone with Cliff, she confides that she's pregnant but has not told Jimmy yet. Later, when Jimmy comes back and Cliff goes out for a while, the couple play their private game of bears and squirrels, using a couple of stuffed toys. Then, Cliff reappears to tell Alison that her old friend Helena Charles is on the phone in the hall. Helena is an actress who has arrived in town with her travelling repertory company and Alison invites her to stay. This news provokes Jimmy into his most vicious rage, a rant in which he wishes that Alison should suffer so that she could become a real human being. This enraged outburst includes a curse on Alison: 'If you could have a child, and it would die [. . .] if only I could watch you face that' (36). The scene ends as he storms out.

Act Two, Scene One

This takes place two weeks later. Alison talks to Helena about how she met Jimmy, how her parents opposed their marriage, and how they manage to live together with Cliff. Helena, who comes from a similar background to Alison's, finds the situation hard to understand. At one point, she asks Alison about her relationship with Cliff, which she finds 'a little strange' because they keep embracing. Alison explains, 'We're simply fond of each other' (40). Helena's questions allow Alison to talk about her and Jimmy's courtship, and how Jimmy and his friend Hugh Tanner, son of Mrs Tanner (who has given Jimmy money to set up his sweet stall), used to gatecrash respectable parties. Alison also suggests that Mrs Tanner blames her for the fact that she never got on with Hugh, who broke with Jimmy soon after his marriage. Alison's fascination with the men's predatory behaviour, and their anti-upper-class attitude, is shared by Helena.

When Cliff and Jimmy arrive, Alison and Helena tell them that they are about to go to church, which sets Jimmy off on an anti-religious outpouring which turns into an attack on Alison's family, and especially on her mother, 'over-fed and a bit flabby' but able to 'bellow like a rhinoceros in labour' (52). He then turns on Helena, accusing her of conspiring against him with his wife. Characterizing her, and others of her class, as 'looking forward to the past' (57), he replies to her threat to slap his face by assuring her that he'd retaliate in the same way. Then he tells her the story of how, when he was ten years old, he watched his father – who had been wounded fighting on the anti-fascist Republican side in the Spanish Civil War – die. When Helena and Alison get up to go, Jimmy feels betrayed by his wife, while she is exhausted by his provocations. Suddenly, there's a phone call for Jimmy. When he leaves to take it, Helena tells Alison that she has sent her parents a telegram, asking them to come and take her home. Alison is too tired to do anything but acquiesce. Jimmy returns: Mrs Tanner has had a stroke, and he decides to go to London to see her before she dies. As Helena and Alison leave for church, Jimmy falls on his bed, devastated by Alison's lack of feeling.

Act Two, Scene Two

This takes place the following evening. Colonel Redfern, Alison's father, has come to take her home. He's a sympathetic character who understands his daughter, and admits that he and his wife were 'not entirely free of blame' (67) in the rift between them and Jimmy. He says that Alison is very similar to himself. But although Redfern cannot really understand Alison's marriage, he is impressed by Jimmy's passion. When Alison tells him that Jimmy calls him 'an old plant left over from the Edwardian Wilderness' (69, 70), he muses nostalgically on his life in India. Alison points out the affinities between him and Jimmy: 'You're hurt because everything is changed. Jimmy is hurt because everything is the same. And neither of you can face it' (70). As Alison packs, she decides to leave her toy squirrel behind.

Then Helena comes in, soon followed by Cliff. She's decided to stay for a while. As Redfern and his daughter exit, Alison leaves a letter for Jimmy with Cliff. After they are gone, he passes it to Helena, saying, 'He's all yours' (75). When Cliff goes out, she plays with Jimmy's stuffed bear. Suddenly, he returns. He has almost been hit by the Redferns' car and is violently angry. Helena gives him Alison's letter and he reacts bitterly. Then she tells him that Alison is pregnant. He turns on her, calling her an 'evil-minded little virgin', and she slaps his face (77). Then she kisses him passionately.

Act Three, Scene One

This scene opens with Jimmy and Cliff reading the Sunday newspapers, while Helena stands at the ironing board. It's several months later, and it soon emerges that although Jimmy's rants about the poverty of intellectual life in Britain are the same as before, a new element has been added: his hatred of Helena's habit of church-going. He taunts her with the idea that they are 'living in sin' (81). As before, Jimmy and Cliff perform loving parodies of music-hall routines and wrestle, although – when Helena goes out – Cliff comments that living with her is 'not the same, is it?' (88). Then he tells Jimmy that he wants to move out, find some different work and a girlfriend of his own. Jimmy reacts by saying that Cliff 'is worth a half dozen Helenas to me' (89), and then launches into a key speech: 'There aren't any good, brave causes left' (89). When Helena returns, and Cliff goes out, the couple's plan to go out for a drink is interrupted by an unexpected arrival: Alison.

Act Three, Scene Two

This scene opens with Alison and Helena talking while Jimmy plays his trumpet in Cliff's room. They explore their feelings for Jimmy, and Alison talks about losing her baby. Helena calls Jimmy back into the room and he realizes what has happened to Alison: 'I don't exactly relish the idea of anyone being ill, or in pain. It was my child too, you know. But (*he shrugs*) it isn't my first loss.' To which Alison replies, 'It was mine' (98). Soon after, Helena – who believes that she has retained her traditional sense of right and wrong – announces her intention to leave. She has had enough of Jimmy's emotional intensity. 'I can't take part – in all this suffering. I can't!' (99). Jimmy reacts by pointing out that 'It's no good trying to fool yourself about love. You can't fall into it like a soft job, without dirtying your hands' (100). As Helena leaves, Jimmy turns on Alison, reminding her that she never sent any flowers to Mrs Tanner's funeral. Then, using the image of the lonely old bear, he appeals to her: 'I may be a lost cause, but I thought that if you loved me, it needn't matter' (101). She responds by joining in with his despair, and telling him about losing their child. As she abases herself, Jimmy realizes that at last she has joined him in his emotional hell. But he can't stand the intensity of the feeling. Instead, he leads them both into the fantasy world of bears and squirrels. As Alison '*slides her arms around him*', the play ends (103).

Character analysis

Jimmy

Like other British dramatists – such as George Bernard Shaw, J. B. Priestley and Terence Rattigan – Osborne gave detailed stage directions at the beginning of his play. *Look Back in Anger*'s anti-hero, Jimmy Porter, 'is a tall, thin young man'. 'He is a disconcerting mixture of sincerity and cheerful malice, of tenderness and freebooting cruelty; restless, importunate, full of pride, a combination which alienates the sensitive and insensitive alike [. . .]. To many he may seem sensitive to the point of vulgarity. To others, he is simply a loudmouth. To be as vehement as he is is to be almost non-committal' (1–2). Clearly this Jimmy is a paradoxical chameleon, hard to pin down. Osborne implies that there is an essential contradiction between his noisy outward character and his quieter inner feelings. Could his pipe smoking, for example, be an outward sign of a confident masculinity that he does not feel? Maybe Jimmy's aggression is a way of concealing his insecurities, doubts and weaknesses.

Since Osborne's intention was 'to make people feel, to give them lessons in feeling' (Maschler, 1957: 65), Jimmy's emotions are central to the play. It's no accident that the chapter on Osborne in Kenneth Allsop's *The Angry Decade* is called 'The Emotionalists'. The core of Jimmy's emotional life – about which he is thrillingly articulate – is the feeling of loss, obviously related to the death of his father. In Jimmy's words, watching his father die taught him at an early age 'what it was to be angry – angry and helpless' (59). The loss taught him not only anger, the central emotion powering the play, but also betrayal – loyalty is Jimmy's core value. It is also significant that he only once mentions his mother (58), although his sense of pain at the death of Mrs Tanner, mother of his estranged friend Hugh, suggests that he craves maternal love. When Cliff talks about Jimmy's sexual experiences, the only one of his previous girlfriends that is discussed is Madeline, who was ten years older than him. In psychological terms, the feminist interpretation that sees Jimmy as a child needing a mother substitute is fairly convincing – especially as Osborne makes sure that Alison loses their child and can thus become a mother to Jimmy.

From the point of view of class, Jimmy's origins are 'from working people' (27), although his university education places him in the lower-middle class, as does his decision to run a sweet stall. Often, he is 'self-consciously proletarian – and self-protectively proud of it. [. . .] The kind of puritanism such a background often breeds – a social rather than a sexual puritanism – is perhaps at the core of Jimmy Porter's character' (Trussler, 1969: 43). His antagonism towards the upper-middle class is based on a conscious rejection of mainstream society – he has dropped out of the world of careers, perhaps because he's afraid of failure. Novelist Anthony Burgess once suggested that, like Dixon in Kingsley Amis's *Lucky Jim* (1954), Jimmy is an example of hypergamy, 'bedding a woman of a social class superior to one's own: this is an aspect of the perennial class motif of British fiction' (Burgess, 1984: 64). Despite the fact that his mother was middle class – she liked 'smart, fashionable' minorities (58) – Jimmy identifies with both the working class and the aristocracy. Feeling uncertain about his own place in the world, he is drawn towards the social classes that seem the most self-confident and self-assured.

Jimmy's nostalgia is not for a world he has lost, but for a world he never had: the political 'good, brave causes' that his father fought for, and the Edwardian era. Looking back, he evokes the latter as a dream, a fantasy, an ideal: 'Always the same picture: high summer, the long days in the sun, slim volumes of verse, crisp linen, the smell of starch'. While he knows rationally that this picture is 'phoney' (11), he needs it as a stable reference point. And, as he himself remarks, it is a sentimental picture. And so is his view of Mrs Tanner. Sentimentality equals stability, and so does fantasy.

For this restless failure of a man, the game of bears and squirrels is not mere whimsy, but answers a profound psychological need. But his relationship with Alison seems only to work on the level of fantasy and sexual play. As Osborne once wrote, Jimmy 'is a young man who is anxious to give a great deal, and is hurt because no one seems interested enough to take it – including his wife' (Osborne, 1957: no page number).

To get security, which means a response that confirms that people are listening to him, Jimmy is endlessly provocative, constantly needling his friends and insulting his enemies. When Cliff sensibly says, 'Don't let's brawl', Jimmy replies: 'Why *don't* we brawl? It's the only thing left I'm any good at' (53). Certainly, Jimmy is a self-centred character: playwright David Edgar comments, 'Jimmy Porter was the first hero of the Me Decade' (Edgar, 1988: 141). In 1991, Osborne remarked that the original perception of Jimmy as an Angry Young Man resulted in 'strident and frequently dull' performances. Instead of noise, Osborne argues for Jimmy as 'a comic character. He generates energy but, also, like, say, Malvolio or Falstaff, an inescapable melancholy. He is a man of gentle susceptibilities, constantly goaded by a brutal and coercive world. This core of character is best expressed, not only theatrically but truthfully, by a *mild* delivery' (Osborne, 1996b: 279–80).

Alison

Osborne describes Alison Porter as an 'elusive personality', about the same age as her husband, and a woman suffering from 'well-bred malaise' (2). Daughter of an upper-middle-class family, she is elegant and, despite Osborne's stipulation that she is 'dark' (2), is often played by a blonde actress (for example, Mary Ure). Alison is well bred, good mannered, and was a virgin when she married Jimmy, to whom she was attracted by the romance of an unsuitable mate. At first sight, she is doing traditional domestic chores, and wearing one of Jimmy's shirts – a sign of her subservience? She certainly endures a whole litany of his complaints: she's too silent; she's unresponsive; she still wants her old friends; she writes letters home to her mother. The central ambiguity in her character is whether she is a silenced victim or a silencing victimizer. How much is her silence a form of passive aggression born out of her own disappointment in life? You get the feeling that she hasn't told Jimmy about her pregnancy not for the reason she gives Cliff – fear of his reaction to new responsibility (26) – but because this secret gives her power.

Like Jimmy, Alison keeps looking back at the past and her childhood. It should be something they share, but they don't. Her father offers his diagnosis: 'I think you may take after me a little, my dear. You like to sit on the fence because it's comfortable and more peaceful' (68). And this is echoed in her softly spoken: 'All I want is a little peace' (60). But Alison, according to Osborne, 'is really incapable of loyalty, even to herself' (Osborne, 1957: n. pag.). Her father realizes that writing letters behind Jimmy's back is a form of betrayal. Certainly, Alison's humiliating return to Jimmy after she has lost the baby involves a grovelling that she, at some level, craves. Yet it is also possible to see Alison as a positive force: 'Hers was in a way a kind of victory; and because it was a kind of victory, it released instead of depressing the spirit' (Hobson, 1984: 190). But, as more than one feminist has pointed out, in the end, 'She has lost her child, just as he wished she would, and with this the possibility of having other children'. Her strength comes at the expense of 'her own gendered identity as a mother in her own right, and her own emotional space' (Wandor, 2001: 46, 47).

Cliff

Osborne describes 25-year-old Cliff Lewis as 'short, dark, big boned [. . .] easy and relaxed, almost to lethargy, with the rather sad, natural intelligence of the self-taught' (2). He's Welsh, of working-class origin, and has not been to university, but is certainly not an ignorant oaf. After all, he manages to hold his own against Jimmy. He's attractive to women, and especially to Alison, and Helena remarks that they are always cuddling and kissing. Although it is clear that their affection is not sexual, Cliff might be slightly in love with her. The key phrase that he uses about his role in the emotional triangle is that he is a 'no-man's land between them' (61). Although frequently overshadowed by the much more provocative Jimmy, Cliff is a vital part of the triangular relationship at the heart of the play, and he adds a sense of stability, and pity, to it. As Osborne said, 'These are two men who care about each other deeply', even if they can't always express it (Osborne, 1957: n. pag.).

Helena

Osborne describes Helena Charles as the same age as Alison, and of 'medium height, carefully and expensively dressed': 'her sense of matriarchal authority makes most men who meet her anxious, not only to please but impress, as if she were the gracious representative of visiting royalty' (37). Clearly upper-middle class, she works as an actress, but differs from Alison in being more self-confident, and being used to receiving respect and admiration from both sexes. Osborne says, 'Life has held no problems for her that could not be solved by a little application and common sense – until she meets Jimmy' (Osborne, 1957: n. pag.). He scorns her as 'this saint in Dior's clothing' (56). Dignified, strong and responsible, she helps Alison with domestic chores, and arranges for Alison's father to collect her and bring her home. This action is deeply ambiguous: is she helping her friend or deliberately trying to get rid of her? Either way, she stands up to Jimmy with greater fortitude than Alison. Perhaps the key to her character is her strong moral sense, expressed both in her church-going, and in her quitting her life of 'sin' (81–2). Clearly, her attraction to Jimmy is an attraction of opposites and the scene in which she first hits, and then kisses, him symbolizes 'the shared sado-masochism of a sexual encounter between social enemies' (Trussler, 1969: 50). However symbolic, it also feels just a little unlikely.

Influences and genre

Look Back in Anger was influenced by Osborne's own life, the general theatre environment of post-war Britain, and, more remotely, by modernist European drama. It is clearly a strongly autobiographical play. In the 'Introduction' to his collected plays, Osborne noted the play's genesis: 'I was a twenty-five-year-old actor, out of work and separated from my first wife. I had been thinking about the play for a year or more and wrote it over a period of six weeks' (Osborne, 1996b: viii).

Osborne's first marriage was a crucial influence on the play. He married Pamela Lane in 1951, but their marriage was in trouble by early 1954, and fell apart that summer. Like Alison, Lane was upper-middle class and the couple's nicknames for each other included 'Teddy', 'Bears', 'Squirrel' and 'Nutty' (Heilpern, 2006: 125). 'Jimmy's courtship of Alison, his dislike of her mother, her family's horror at the news of their engagement, their hiring of a private detective to stalk him, his descriptions of their wedding and the current state of their marriage, are all inspired by Osborne's life with Pamela' (Whitebrook, 2005). In Osborne's autobiography, his life with Lane is illustrated by quotations from *Look Back in Anger*. John Heilpern, Osborne's official biographer, records that when Lane saw the play soon after it opened, 'she had the surreal experience' of seeing her marriage 'reinvented onstage'. '"Oh, no," she remembered thinking with a sense of dread even as the curtain rose. "Not the ironing board"' (Heilpern, 2006: 123).

Similarly, Osborne's anti-hero Jimmy is a fantasy image of himself, a feeling person who is able to articulate his frustrations in well-written speeches. Indeed, in the England of the 1950s – where expressions of feeling were frowned on and a stiff upper lip preferred – Osborne's desire to express emotions was seen as a radical act. Kenneth Tynan praised Jimmy's refusal 'to accept "emotional" as a term of abuse' (Tynan, 2007: 113). There is further evidence that Osborne's personal life spilled over into the play. Novelist Angus Wilson – whose *The Mulberry Bush* was also staged at the Royal Court in 1956 – archly remembered that he thought the play's characters 'were really rather strongly reminiscent of the members of a provincial repertory company' (Griffiths, 1981: 6–7). But although the emotional fuel of the play came from Osborne's personal experience, and especially his sense of having been betrayed by Lane (Heilpern, 2006: 129), the form his play took was influenced by the theatre environment of post-war Britain.

British theatre in the early 1950s still bore the stamp of the 1920s. It was dominated by what Tynan satirically dubbed 'the Loamshire play'. In a 1954 article headlined 'Apathy', Tynan characterized the genre as genteel upper-class country-house dramas, light comedies or predictable thrillers, and all written in the clipped language of the upper-middle class. This 'glibly codified fairy-tale world' was unable to reflect the fast-changing social realities of the post-war period. 'There is nothing in the London theatre', he argued, 'that one dares to discuss with an intelligent man for more than five minutes' (Tynan, 2007: 36–7). It was, as visiting American playwright Arthur Miller said, a theatre 'hermetically sealed against the way the society moves' (Marowitz *et al.*, 1965: 40). Theatre audiences, led by what Terence Rattigan called Aunt Ednas, wore evening dress, and could, during matinees, have tea and cake delivered to their seats. In a theatre dominated by the late work of craftsmen such as Noël Coward and Terence Rattigan, the well-made play was king. Its form was the traditional one of a beginning, a middle and an end, with strong curtain lines at the end of each of three acts. It was a drama that depended on revelations and reversals, with a satisfying coherence of form, a recognizable social setting and a pervasive feeling that justice had been done to all the characters.

Osborne knew the work of both Rattigan and Coward through acting in their plays in repertory theatre productions. But although his grandfather predicted that he would be the next Shaw, he disliked the playwright, remarking that 'Shaw avoided passion almost as prudently as Coward' (Osborne, 1991: 257). At one point in *Look Back in Anger*, Osborne mentions a 'proper little Marchbanks' (12), an allusion to Shaw's 1897 play *Candida*, which aptly enough is as much about male chauvinism as about philistinism. In view of the fact that Coward and Rattigan were driven off the stage by the advent of the New Wave, it is somewhat ironic that Coward's 1925 play, *Hay Fever*, has a speech about 'feeling', when Myra accuses the Blisses of not having 'one sincere or genuine feeling among the lot of you' (56). During the course of his career, Osborne developed a great deal of respect for the craft of Coward and Rattigan. Other British predecessors of *Look Back in Anger* include plays that dealt with the theme of upper-class gals falling for unsuitable boys, in work such as *The Fugitive* (1913) by John Galsworthy and *The Best People* (1926) by David Grey and Avery Hopwood. Another clear influence is the British tradition of music-hall acts, whose song and dance routines and saucy double meanings are parodied in the play. Osborne adored the work of vaudeville performers such as Max Miller, an admiration that comes across in his portrait of Archie Rice in *The Entertainer*.

When Osborne was collaborating with Stella Linden, she told him he needed a 'short sharp lesson in Pinero' (Osborne, 1981: 195). By this, she meant that he needed to understand the genre of the well-made three-act play. Developed by nineteenth-century French dramatists such as Eugène Scribe and Victorien Sardou, this form cultivated suspense by using dramatic irony and withheld information. In theatre terms, the three-act play often involved two intervals, which was good for sales of refreshments. The three acts comprised exposition, complication and dénouement. Osborne evidently took Linden's advice. Act One of *Look Back in Anger* introduces the main characters and finishes on a strong curtain line as Jimmy curses Alison (dramatic irony). In Act Two, complications are introduced as Helena, a new character, arrives and Alison leaves, without telling Jimmy that she's pregnant (withheld information). It ends on a dramatic high as Helena hits and kisses Jimmy. In Act Three, after an ironic reprise of the start of Act One, Cliff decides to leave, Helena realizes that she can't stay, and Alison returns. The curtain falls on Jimmy and Alison embracing. As regards its form, Osborne's ironic sally that *Look Back in Anger* was 'a formal, rather old fashioned play' had an essential kernel of truth (Taylor, 1968: 66). The use of Alison's pregnancy as a dramatic device also brings to mind Barney, the cynical agent of *Epitaph for George Dillon*, whose advice is: 'get someone in the family way in the Third Act – you're halfway there' (Osborne, 1996b: 168; cf. 326).

In genre terms, *Look Back in Anger* is thus a well-made play in which conflicts are introduced and then resolved, themes suggested and then reprised. In Act One, Helena disrupts domestic harmony; in Act Three, Alison does the same. From the point of view of realism, the first act is perfectly convincing but the Act Two scene between Alison and Helena is markedly less realistic, in that Osborne is using the fact that they have not seen much of each other since Alison got married to articulate the backstory of Jimmy's character, and of his relationship with Alison. In Act Two, in order to catch the curtain, Helena kisses Jimmy a bit too quickly for strict realism. In Act Three, her decision to leave is equally rapid, and equally forced. There is, however, a sense of dramatic development in that Helena's response to Jimmy is different from Alison's, but there is also a rush of loose ends being tidied up as she decides to leave when Alison reappears. In the final moments, there's a feeling that both Jimmy and Alison have been changed by their experiences. *Look Back in Anger* may not exactly be a piece of 'straightforward dramatic realism, but with an emphasis on people rather than on plot', but that is certainly how it struck many people at the time (Banham, 1969: 12). As Ronald Duncan, another victim of the New Wave, observed, 'The so-called "kitchen-sink" dramatists are still writing within the convention of [Pinero's] *Mrs Tanqueray*' – 'but to invert a convention is not to break it' (Taylor, 1968: 192).

Finally, some aspects of *Look Back in Anger* reflect a wider European theatre culture, elements of which were, in their time, radical and modernistic. A few reviewers of the original production, for example, noticed a Strindbergian element in Osborne's portrait of a marriage. In work such as *Miss Julie* (1888) and *The Dance of Death* (1900), Swedish playwright August Strindberg gave vent to his own intense but often confused feelings about women by showing sexual relations and marriage as a deadly struggle between male and female. Hell is married people. Such mixed feelings, of love and hate, are an essential ingredient of Osborne's play.

Despite all these influences, it is worth stressing that what distinguished *Look Back in Anger* was its lower-class setting and the vitality of its language. But while Osborne's language sounds like simple naturalism, it is in fact highly coloured and exaggerated speech, even when it sounds colloquial and ordinary. As Osborne himself said, 'The language which actors were called upon to speak when I first began work was thin and inexpressive.' But his language was not mere naturalism because 'the language of "everyday life" is almost incommunicable for the very good reason that it is restricted, inarticulate, dull and boring' (Osborne, 1996b: x). What was new, of course, was Osborne's tone of voice. His language was a fired up and eloquent version of familiar talk. His flights of rhetoric are the

imaginary speech of conflicts recollected in anything but tranquillity. Yet the play, he insisted, was a comedy: 'A performance of *Look
Back* without persistent laughter is like an opera without arias.
Indeed, Jimmy Porter's inaccurately named "tirades" should be
approached as arias, and require the most adroit handling, delicacy
of delivery, invention and timing' (Osborne, 1996b: x–xi).

Close reading of key scenes

Act One: 'Hallelujah! I'm alive!'

Look Back in Anger opens in an atmosphere of boredom. It's early
evening on a rainy Sunday in a 1950s Midland town. The fact that
Osborne specifies April suggests T. S. Eliot's opening line from *The
Waste Land* (1922): 'April is the cruellest month' (Eliot, 1960: 27).
In the play, Jimmy mentions Eliot twice (50, 83). The slow
opening of the play, with the thud of Alison's ironing, the rustling
of the newspapers and the disconnected dialogue creates an atmosphere of claustrophobia and hopelessness. In the 1950s, most shops
would have been shut on Sunday, and the only thing to do in the
evening would have been to go to the cinema or pub. In BBC
radio's *Hancock's Half Hour*, the comedian Tony Hancock parodied
this in episodes such as 'Sunday Afternoon at Home' and 'The East
Cheam Drama Festival' (both April 1958).

At first, Jimmy is irritated, nagging and petulant, demanding tea
and then refusing it (5, 8), like 'a child' says Alison (19). Although
he tries to provoke Alison by suggesting that her father, 'Daddy',
wrote a reactionary letter to the newspaper, she is lost in her own
thoughts. The stage directions say she talks '*absently*' (3) or '*without
looking up*' (5). Her most typical utterance is an exasperated
'Jimmy, for heaven's sake! I can't think!' (4). By contrast, Cliff is
quick to defend her and – in response to Jimmy – he gives as good
as he gets. Their banter is good-natured: when Cliff compares
Jimmy's appetite for food to that of a 'sexual maniac', and parodies

a *News of the World* newspaper story about him being arrested and 'pleading guilty to interfering with a small cabbage and two tins of beans', Jimmy's response is eloquent: he '*grins*' (4). He appreciates Cliff's playfulness. But his response is also significant: 'I like to eat. I'd like to live too' (4). Note how the first sentence is a statement of fact and the second conditional. Jimmy would like to live but he can't. He's being held back. Osborne is preparing the ground for Jimmy's first significant outburst.

It's boredom that sparks things off. Cooped up in one room, Jimmy, Alison and Cliff are always getting on each other's nerves. Jimmy, of course, is the first to complain: 'God, how I hate Sundays! It's always so depressing, always the same. We never seem to get any further, do we? Always the same ritual' (8). He emphasizes his point by the repetition of 'always' and 'the same'. And his rhetorical question is typically vague. He doesn't quite know how to articulate his idea yet. But Cliff unwittingly helps him out when he suggests that they go to the cinema. Alison says she can't and then turns to Jimmy: 'Would you like to?' (8). It's an apparently innocent question, but Jimmy's response is typically antagonistic:

And have my enjoyment ruined by the Sunday night yobs in the front row? No, thank you. (*pause*) Did you read Priestley's piece this week? Why on earth I ask I don't know. I know damned well you haven't. Why do I spend ninepence on that damned paper every week? Nobody reads it except me. Nobody can be bothered. No one can raise themselves out of their delicious sloth. You two will drive me round the bend soon – I know it, as sure as I'm sitting here. I know you're going to drive me mad. Oh heavens, how I long for a little ordinary human enthusiasm. Just enthusiasm – that's all. I want to hear a warm, thrilling voice cry out Hallelujah! (*He bangs his breast theatrically.*) Hallelujah! I'm alive! I've an idea. Why don't we have a little game? Let's pretend that we're human beings, and that we're actually alive.

Just for a while. What do you say? Let's pretend we're human. (*He looks from one to the other.*) Oh, brother, it's such a long time since I was with anyone who got enthusiastic about anything. (8–9)

The first line of Jimmy's rant, which begins as a rejection of Alison's suggestion, emphasizes the fact that Jimmy, for all his anti-upper-class opinions, is a bit of a snob. He's no teenage rock 'n' roller. He shows off his education whenever he can. His reference to the writer and playwright J. B. Priestley stresses what he perceives to be the difference between him and his friends: he cares and they don't. Indeed, he soon returns to Priestley with a scornful 'He's like Daddy – still casting well-fed glances back to the Edwardian twilight', a food metaphor in which Jimmy's hunger for life is implicitly contrasted with the complacency of a well-fed Establishment (9).

In his set speeches, Jimmy uses his rhetorical skills to good effect to bang home his point, as with his repetition of 'nobody', followed by the variation 'no one'. His repetition of 'damned' is an echo of his earlier 'damn you, damn both of you, damn them all' (8), a response to Cliff's indifference to his 'God, how I hate Sundays!' speech. And the phrase 'delicious sloth' illustrates his enjoyment in haranguing his captive audience. Such eloquence is a good example of how Osborne's dialogue goes beyond simple naturalism.

The next two phrases, about being driven mad, show Jimmy's typical soapbox exaggeration, until he finally reaches his goal, his manifesto for living: 'Oh heavens, how I long for a little ordinary human enthusiasm.' But his immediate illustration of this idea is anything but ordinary. The 'warm, thrilling voice' that cries 'Hallelujah!' is a reference to black gospel music, and a subliminal reminder that he once had a jazz band and still plays the trumpet, usually as a way of asserting himself. It is possible to guess what was on Osborne's mind by comparing this line with a longer passage from *The Entertainer*, where Archie Rice talks about his own moment of epiphany: 'If I ever saw any hope or strength in the human race, it was in the face of that old fat negress getting up to sing about Jesus' (Osborne, 1961: 70). In a rather Orientalist way, Osborne sees the black blues or gospel singer as the embodiment of 'natural' humanity (Osborne, 1961: 71). In *Look Back in Anger*, this is merely hinted at, but Jimmy is explicit about what he values: 'Hallelujah! I'm alive!' As Dan Rebellato points out, in the cultural politics of the 1950s, '"Life" is the crucial word. It is part of a cluster of terms that are distributed equally through the works of the New Left and the New Wave: the variant forms, "live", "living", "alive", the antonyms, "dead", "death", the synonyms, "vital" and "vitality", and the related term "feeling"' (Rebellato, 1999: 21). Osborne's supporters, such as Tynan, made it clear that 'Jimmy is simply and abundantly alive' (Tynan, 2007: 113). But if Jimmy is alive, this implies that Alison and Cliff are, if not dead, at least slow, sleepy and slothful. Just as Osborne wanted to give lessons in feeling, so Jimmy wants others to feel what he feels.

When Jimmy, by now in full flight, suggests that 'we have a little game', it's interesting that he uses the verb 'to have' rather than the more usual 'to play' as in 'Why don't we *play* a little game?' Suddenly, there's nothing very playful about Jimmy: his 'Let's pretend that we're human beings, and that we're actually alive' is in deadly earnest, and when '*He looks from one to the other*' it's a glare of accusation. And his final punch, 'it's such a long time since I was with anyone who got enthusiastic about anything', is directed squarely at Alison, as the next stage direction makes clear: when Cliff changes the subject, Jimmy is '*resentful of being dragged away from his pursuit of Alison*' (9). So, in this speech, there is a psychological and verbal pattern: Jimmy starts with a rebuff to his wife, then broadens his attack on both his friends, before refocusing once again on Alison. But his attitude to life and sloth is not purely declamatory – they lie at the heart of the play's plot.

At the end of Act One, provoked by news of the arrival of Helena, Jimmy finally turns on Alison with a speech of unmitigated savagery:

Oh, my dear wife, you've got so much to learn. I only hope you learn it one day. If only something – something would happen to you, and wake you out of your beauty sleep! (*coming in close to her*) If you could have a child and it would die. Let it grow, let a recognisable human face emerge from that little mass of indiarubber and wrinkles. (*She retreats away from him.*) Please – if only I could watch you face that. I wonder if you might even become a recognisable human being yourself. But I doubt it. (36)

To qualify as a human being, Alison must – according to her husband – suffer loss, just as he has suffered the loss of his father, and later of Mrs Tanner. From this loss comes his anger, and his idea of being enthusiastic, alive, human. His curse on Alison, which carries strong dramatic irony because while the audience already knows she's pregnant, he doesn't, is visceral. His idea of a foetus as a 'little mass of indiarubber and wrinkles' also suggests an unconscious thought about her father, who has served in India and is wrinkled with age. And his application of the idea of a recognizable human being to his wife implies that she hasn't been born yet. And, if she isn't fully human, it's acceptable for him to abuse her.

Clearly, his attacks are fuelled by a general contempt for women. In November 1956, Osborne wrote a provocative *Daily Mail* article, 'What's Gone Wrong with Women?', in which he claimed that his anger was 'due to the fact that we are becoming dominated by female values, and by the characteristic female indifference to anything but immediate, personal suffering' (Osborne, 1994: 256). As the New Left's Stuart Hall wrote in 1961, Osborne tries to 'burn his way into that tangled subliminal area where the issues of politics and the issues of love and sex merge, mingle and collide'. Jimmy strips away cliché and cant until 'he reaches that inner core where people either "feel" or are irretrievably "dead". The dead thing which drives Jimmy to distraction within Alison [. . .] is also the dead heart of England' (Hall, 1965b: 217). In answer to the play's original critics, it doesn't matter what Jimmy's angry about – what matters is that he is angry, that he feels, that he's alive. By the end of Act One, Jimmy has shown – through helplessness, anger and cruelty – ample evidence of Osborne's 'blazing determination to bring human emotion back into the centre of cultural life' (Rebellato, 1999: 32).

Act Two: 'A question of allegiances'

At the start of Act Two, Helena asks Alison why she married Jimmy (43). Her family, she replies, had just returned from India, and she was innocent: 'I didn't know I was born as Jimmy says' (44), a reference to his cursing of her at the end of Act One. She met Jimmy at a party; he had arrived by bicycle. While everyone else saw him as 'a rather odd creature', Alison was drawn to him: 'Everything about him seemed to burn, his face, the edges of his hair glistened and seemed to spring off his head, and his eyes were so blue and full of the sun. He looked so young and frail, in spite of the tired line of his mouth' (44). Alison swings between seeing Jimmy and his friend Hugh as rapacious gatecrashers, 'barbarian' invaders – 'plundering them, wolfing their food and drinks, and smoking their cigars like ruffians' (43) – and seeing Jimmy as a knight in shining armour, 'except that his armour didn't really shine very much' (44). The correction is typical of her acute self-awareness. With Helena, Alison is conscious of the difficulty of her relationship with Jimmy, and Osborne makes her struggle to articulate his code of values: 'It isn't easy to explain. It's what he would call a question of allegiances, and he expects you to be pretty literal about them' (40). According to her, Jimmy expects loyalty not only to himself, but also to the ideas he believes in, his friends, his former lovers and even his past. When, at the end of the scene, Alison decides to go to church with Helena rather than to Mrs Tanner's bedside with Jimmy, he sees it as a betrayal, and one which justifies his further humiliation of her.

At the same time, Jimmy is passionately attracted to Alison. Here, Osborne turns the claustrophobia of the Porters' cramped living space into a crucible of desire. After he admits that he hurt her 'on purpose' by barging into the ironing board, he says, 'There's hardly a moment when I'm not – watching and wanting you. I've got to hit out somehow. Nearly four years of being in the same room with you, night and day, and I still can't stop my sweat breaking out when I see you doing – something as ordinary as leaning over an ironing board' (30–1). Osborne's idea of Jimmy's contradictions is clearly brought out in the way he slides from looking and desiring Alison to wanting to lash out. Note that he describes his verbal aggression as 'hitting out'. The quick shifts in his character from love to hate are evident soon after when he explains to Cliff why he is searching Alison's handbag: 'Living night and day with another human being has made me predatory and suspicious' (35). The phrase 'night and day' joins these two speeches, the one ostensibly loving and lustful, the other suspicious and anxious. Jimmy embodies Osborne's contradictory feelings about women.

Alison's description of Jimmy as 'so young and frail' is also an echo of something she said to Cliff in Act One, the only time that anyone in the play actually alludes to its title: 'I keep looking back, as far as I remember, and I can't think what it was to feel young, really young. Jimmy said the same thing to me the other day' (24). Alison's attraction to Jimmy is not just that of a well-brought-up young woman to an unsuitable boy – both also share a sense of lost childhood. This feeling is at the root of the bears-and-squirrels game. After they married, Jimmy and Alison shared a flat with

Hugh, but that ended when he went abroad. Alison explains that the game 'was the one way of escaping from everything – a sort of unholy priesthole of being animals to one another. We could become little furry creatures with little furry brains. [. . .] A silly symphony for people who couldn't bear the pain of being human beings any longer' (46). The game of fluffy animals means that Alison and Jimmy have a place to express uncomplicated affection for each other, like children. It's an escape from the 'pain of being human beings'.

If Jimmy and Cliff's relationship is unproblematic, the relationship between Alison and Cliff is odd. Following the tenderness they express towards one another in their normal daily routine – in Act One Cliff '*kisses her hand, and puts her fingers in his mouth*' (6) – Cliff bandages her arm when she gets burnt by the iron. Here, he acts like a father to her, but both of them are mutually dependent on each other. Noticing the physical expressions of their tenderness, Helena can't believe they are 'simply fond of each other'. Alison says, 'You mean there must be something physical too? I suppose there is, but it's not exactly a consuming passion', more a 'relaxed cheerful sort of thing'. Helena is aghast that 'anyone's that lazy' (40). Alison claims that she and Cliff are more interested in the calm they enjoy through restraint than the passion they might experience through sex. In this way, Osborne proves that Jimmy's accusation that they both suffer from 'delicious sloth' is quite right. They can't be bothered to embrace life. Their play-acting of sensible father and sweet girl is as much a retreat from reality as Jimmy and Alison's bears-and-squirrels game.

Jimmy treats women roughly, but his attitude to homosexuals is, by the standards of the 1950s, an odd mix of tolerance and provocation. That the two things are related is clear from his reaction to news of Helena's arrival: 'I've just about had enough of this "expense of spirit" lark, as far as women are concerned. Honestly, it's enough to make you become a schoolmaster or something isn't it? Sometimes I almost envy old Gide and the Greek Chorus Boys' (34). The reference is to Shakespeare's sonnet 'Th' expense of spirit in a waste of shame/Is lust in action' (no. 129). Despite the 'hell' of being homosexual, in a society which saw it as a crime, 'plenty of them seem to have a revolutionary fire' (34). Although you could object that here Jimmy glamorizes gays, he also says that Webster appreciates him because 'I refuse to treat him either as a clown or as a tragic hero' (34), two of the ways that gays were portrayed on the stage at the time. The play, as Dan Rebellato points out, embodies Osborne's complex attitude to homosexuals: 'homosexuality threads through this play, structurally, as a kind of organiser of narrative, and thematically as an ongoing concern of the characters' (Rebellato, 1999: 219).

But what gets Jimmy really going is women and especially upper-class women. And, of course, the archetypal mother-in-law. This is clear from his attacks on Alison's mother. When Jimmy realizes that Alison is going to church with Helena, his sense of being betrayed awakens and he hits out at her mother, calling her a liar, cheat and blackmailer, 'a rhinoceros in labour', 'over-fed and flabby', and finally: 'she's an old bitch and should be dead' (52–3). Jimmy's attack on Alison's mother culminates in an image of her death that mixes imagery from the Jacobean playwright John Webster with contemporary references: 'my God, those worms will need a good dose of salts the day they get through her! [. . .] She will pass away, my friends, leaving a trail of worms gasping for laxatives' (53–4). He describes his wedding as a defeat for Alison's mother: 'the noble, female rhino, pole-axed at last!' (55). But his contempt for older women also colours his declaration that one day 'I may write a book about us all [. . .] and it won't be recollected in tranquillity either, picking daffodils with Auntie Wordsworth' (54). Was this an unconscious repost to Rattigan's Aunt Edna? Mothers and aunties are fair game. Jimmy's declaration that his memoirs will be written 'in fire, and blood. My blood' (54) sounds almost biblical, and is a distant echo of the climax of J. B. Priestley's *An Inspector Calls*: 'If men will not learn that lesson, then they will be taught it in fire and blood' (Priestley, 1969: 207). Like 'life', 'blood' is a key word: in his relentless pursuit of Alison, Jimmy has '*got to draw blood somehow*' (15), '*he can smell blood again*' (56) and '*he's drawn blood at last*' (60). Act Three opens with Jimmy's satire on satanic orgies, in which people drink 'the blood of a white cockerel' (79), a 'satanic' joke he refers back to in his final speech to Alison (103). You can see why Tynan characterized their marriage as 'each with its teeth sunk deep into the other's neck, and each reluctant to break the clinch for fear of bleeding to death' (Tynan, 2007: 112).

Act Three: 'When we were still kids'

Blood also features in Jimmy's most famous speech. In Act Three, Scene One, he says, '*in his familiar, semi-serious mood*', 'There aren't any good, brave causes left.' This recapitulates the previous line in which he declares: 'I suppose people of our generation aren't able to die for good causes any longer. We had all that done for us, in the thirties and forties, when we were still kids' (89). This speech echoes Jimmy's Act One idea that homosexuals 'seem to have a cause' (34) and raises once more a theme which recurs throughout the play: the past and its hold over the present. Jimmy constantly sees himself as trapped between a past which can only be looked back at and a present which is unfulfilling. But his idealized vision of the past only reminds him of the poverty of ideals in the present. Emotionally, the past releases in him feelings that have nowhere to go, and thus turn into senseless aggression. This aggression is aimed at women. This speech, for example, begins: 'Why, why, why, why, do we let these women bleed us dry', and ends in a similar vein: 'No, there's nothing left for it, me boy, but to let yourself be butchered by the women' (89). As well as exemplifying the imagery of blood, this litany of whys echoes Alison's desperate cry in Act Two Scene One: 'Why, why, why, why! [. . .] That word's pulling my head off!' (55). So the political idea that 'There aren't any good, brave causes left' is sandwiched between two highly rhetorical and declamatory attacks on womanhood. And both are strong echoes of the curtain line to Act One: 'She'll go on sleeping and devouring me until there's nothing left of me' (36). In these Strindbergian speeches, women are seen as bloodsuckers of male vitality and annihilators of male potency.

But if Jimmy's attitude to women feels emotionally genuine, his attitude to politics is less straightforward. Of course, the no 'good, brave causes' speech was hailed in the late 1950s as a sign of the reawakened liberal conscience, an example of what Tynan called Jimmy's 'instinctive leftishness' (Tynan, 2007: 113). Yet, even at the time, Osborne warned against taking Jimmy's rhetoric too literally: in 'They Call It Cricket', he wrote, 'It is too simple to say that Jimmy Porter himself believed that there are no good, brave causes left' (Maschler, 1957: 69). And, looking back from old age, Osborne said that the Establishment of the 1950s was so absurdly old-fashioned that 'it made life easy for the liberal conscience' (Osborne, 1991: 3). Certainly Jimmy's liberal passions only really take off when there is some emotional fuel behind then, usually derived from his anger about Alison and her family. His attack on her brother Nigel as the 'Platitude from Outer Space' (14) neatly mixes marital frustration with class hatred.

But looking back at 'good, brave causes' also smacks of nostalgia. Time after time, the past exerts its hold on Jimmy. It is one key to his character. Jimmy is angry not only because that is his way of coping with the confusion of the present, but also because he experiences the present as precarious, full of potential betrayals and agonizing emotions. By contrast, his idea of the past is that of a stable, idealized and sentimentalized condition. Hence Jimmy's grudging respect for Colonel Redfern: both men find the past a place of safe stability. After conjuring up a 'romantic picture' of the

Edwardian twilight, Jimmy says: 'If you've no world of your own, it's rather pleasant to regret the passing of someone else's. I must be getting sentimental' (11). Quite. But each of Jimmy's relationships is anchored by the ballast of the past. With Madeline, his former (older) lover, Jimmy uses an idealized past to criticize an impoverished present: at the slothful Alison and Cliff, he spits, 'She had more animation in her little finger than you two put together' (13). Because she is safely in the past, Madeline can be perfection. Also, in stark contrast to his image of the present as 'About as pointless and inglorious as stepping in front of a bus' (89), Jimmy remembers Madeline as being so 'awake' and 'curious' that 'Even to sit on the top of a bus with her was like setting out with Ulysses' (13). In this subliminal way, past adventures contrast with present threats.

Jimmy's memories of his own past, whether they are of Hugh or of Mrs Tanner, are idealized and solid. When Alison returns in Act Three, Helena reiterates Jimmy's alienation from the present in terms of the past: 'There's no place for people like that any longer – in sex, or politics, or anything. That's why he's so futile. Sometimes, when I listen to him, I feel he thinks he's still in the middle of the French Revolution' (96). Alison agrees: 'I suppose he's what you'd call an Eminent Victorian' (96). As she instantly realizes, this is a repeat of their previous conversation about Jimmy. The emotional origin of Jimmy's constant looking back is, of course, the death of his father as a result of the Spanish Civil War, an example of noble suffering in a 'good, brave' cause. Earlier, he contrasts his uncaring mother's attitude to his father with his own feelings: 'But *I* was the only one who cared'. 'You see,' he continues, 'I learnt at an early age what it was to be angry and helpless'. Significantly, the experience also taught him about 'betrayal' (59). But while his anger is apparent throughout the play, at the end it is his helplessness that is most evident. What Jimmy wants from Alison is not a wife but, in her words, 'a kind of cross between a mother and a Greek courtesan, a henchwoman, a mixture of Cleopatra and

Boswell' (97). In the end, the only way to escape the 'pain of being alive' (100), the adult relationship of a man and a woman, is to retreat into a fantasy world as stable and as powerful as that of an idealized past: the game of bears and squirrels. The bruising contradictions of the couple's love and hate are resolved not in the real world, but in the world of fantasy. Fiction heals what reality cannot. It is, after all, a play.

Changing views of the play

Look Back in Anger has always been controversial. In 1968, John Russell Taylor introduced the first collection of critical viewpoints about the play by saying that John Osborne and his work 'are interesting to us now as much for what they stand for as for what they are' (Taylor, 1968: 11). Indeed, the first commentators looked mainly at how the play managed to capture the mood of its time, its zeitgeist. For Taylor, the play was not just a success, but also the advent of a phenomenon: 'If ever a revolution began with one explosion it was this' (Taylor, 1969: 14). The revolution in postwar British theatre – where the vapid, genteel country-house comedies were replaced by gritty, brash and politically relevant social realist drama – started with Osborne. What made the play revolutionary was not innovation in its form, but in its content and in the directness of the language through which it was expressed (Taylor, 1969: 40). When analysing the play itself, Taylor was conscious of Jimmy's psychological deficiencies: 'There are constant indications of his neurotic determination to establish and keep his supremacy in any situation, inventing trouble if there is none lying around to do so, his hysterical persecution of Alison, his childish petulance' (Taylor, 1969: 44). Yet Taylor also points out that, on stage, Jimmy comes across much more positively. By casting 'stocky, substantial, heroic figures' – actors such as Kenneth Haigh and Richard Burton – instead of 'weedy neurotics', Jimmy becomes a 'saintlike witness to right values in a world gone wrong, the mouthpiece of protest for a dissatisfied generation' (Taylor, 1969: 44). The performance adds meaning to the text.

Most early analyses focused on the nature of the Angry Young Man, a mix of John Osborne and Jimmy Porter turned into a figure that represents an era. Although this could be seen as an example of the biographical fallacy, in which the life of the author is confused with the life of his fictions, in this case it seems perfectly justifiable. On BBC's *Panorama* programme on 9 July 1956, Osborne seemed to accept the 'tag' of Angry Young Man (Ritchie, 1988: 27) and, in 1957, he wrote that if people had heard of him it was 'only as a rather odd-looking "angry young man"' (Maschler, 1957: 64), an echo of a phrase used by Alison about Jimmy: 'this rather odd creature' (44).

It is also clear that early reactions to *Look Back in Anger* were influenced by the critic F. R. Leavis. As Katherine J. Worth pointed out in 1963, the play is not just about the generation gap, but also about the feelings and expressiveness of one individual, Jimmy. Jimmy's tirades are not motivated by commitment to a political cause, but are the expression – 'at the same time violent and controlled, sardonically humorous and deadly earnest' (Worth, 1968: 103) – of his anger. But what is he angry about? He is outraged by 'the lack of imaginative response' (Worth, 1968: 104) to the world's suffering, whether it is his own, his father's or Mrs Tanner's. This 'imaginative suffering', argues Worth, is a 'profoundly solitary experience' (Worth, 1968: 105). Jimmy is 'a suffering hero, and the action is designed to illuminate his suffering rather than to force a conflict' (Worth, 1968: 106). Here, Leavisite notions of life, vitality and felt experience mingle in a highly sympathetic account. Osborne becomes an example of what Leavis called 'a vital capacity for experience, a kind of reverent openness before life, and a marked moral intensity' (Leavis, 1962: 17). Such attitudes were widespread. In 1959, for example, Stuart Hall said that the play 'contained something of our sense of life' and 'gave us lessons in feeling' (Hall, 1965a: 115).

Similar notions of life and vitality, exemplified in Jimmy's 'Hallelujah! I'm alive' speech (9), also pervaded the debate. In 1957, director Lindsay Anderson, for example, advocated 'vital theatre' and the notion of 'commitment' in *Encore*, a theatre magazine whose subtitle was 'The Voice of Vital Theatre' (Anderson, 1965: 47). Then, in a letter defending his article, he quoted Leavis's *Scrutiny* (Anderson, 1965: 51). 'Vital' denoted energy, urgency and youth. Commitment – articulated by Anderson in his *Sight and Sound* essay 'Stand Up! Stand Up!' – is the political aspect of the Leavisite notion of 'moral intensity'. This mixed a soft version of the Marxist-Leninist idea of a vanguard party leading social reform with a puritan notion of moral renewal, and gave a passing nod to Jean-Paul Sartre's idea of being *engagé*. In the 1950s, the idea of moral protest seemed to be a good response to what was widely perceived to be a hypocritical and incompetent Establishment. In 1961, however, John Mander criticized Osborne by turning the playwright's comment about Jimmy – 'To be as vehement as he is is to be almost non-committal' – against the author himself (Mander, 1968: 149). Commitment was an important preoccupation of early audiences.

But there are other ways of seeing the play. A cultural materialist analysis of *Look Back in Anger* would stress the original conditions of production – the Royal Court's state subsidy (which rose from £7,000 in 1956 to £20,000 in 1962, and then £50,000 in 1965) and its ideology of the Right to Fail – and could compare the play with other discourses which also articulated opposition to the Establishment. In 1957, for example, Tom Maschler edited *Declaration*, a collection of essays by Osborne, Tynan, Anderson, Doris Lessing and Colin Wilson. They all addressed ideas about commitment, freedom in a conformist society, fear of the atom bomb, and the problem of leisure. They explored the question of what to believe and how to act in the context of a consumer society: as Maschler pointed out, 'anger has become a highly saleable commodity' (Maschler, 1957: 8). There was a hunger for these ideas: *Declaration* 'sold the astonishing total of twenty-five thousand copies in the first three months' (Allsop, 1958: 124). Among such texts, Jimmy's speeches are part of a widespread feeling that due to the moral failure of the previous generation there had, in Robert Hewison's words, 'been some kind of cultural collapse' (Hewison, 1988: 159). They seem less like personal neurosis and more like a particular expression of widely held views about Britain's changing place in the world.

But some writers took a much more literary approach. In 1959, the novelist Mary McCarthy, one of Osborne's earliest American champions, compared his play to another at the heart of English culture: Shakespeare's *Hamlet*. Tynan had made the same connection, calling Jimmy 'the completest young pup in our literature since Hamlet' (Tynan, 2007: 112). McCarthy sees Jimmy as Hamlet, Cliff as his loyal Horatio, and Alison as Ophelia. 'The scenes Jimmy makes with Alison have the same candid brutality that Hamlet showed to Ophelia' and 'Both Hamlet and Jimmy Porter have declared war upon a rotten society. Both have been unfitted by a higher education from accepting their normal place in the world. They think too much and criticize freely.' Alison's mother is, absurdly, Polonius (McCarthy, 1968: 154). Interestingly, Osborne had played Hamlet once, drunkenly, as an actor at the Victoria Theatre, Hayling Island, in 1950, and he always kept an edition of the play 'where he had crossed out all the other parts leaving Hamlet to go it alone' (Heilpern, 2006: 171). But comparing *Look Back in Anger* with *Hamlet* is an example of decontextualized criticism – such as that of I. A. Richards's New Criticism – in which texts can be compared without any historical background, purely as examples of writing which elicit true judgement based on firsthand opinion. However insightful, the limitations of this approach are obvious.

By the late 1960s, there were several accounts of Osborne's work which, if theoretically modest, did underline important themes. In 1969, Simon Trussler rightly pointed out that 'the biographical fallacy' has been 'the most persistent obstacle to a better understanding of his work' (Trussler, 1969: 13–14). Trussler saw *Look Back in Anger* as already 'a myth' (Trussler, 1969: 40), a suggestive phrase that evokes French semiotician Roland Barthes' work on cultural icons, *Mythologies* (a book which was originally published the year after the play's premiere). Trussler emphasized that 'before the myth-makers got to work' (Trussler, 1969: 45), the play's themes were class war, nostalgia, and the compensatory quality of Jimmy and Alison's bears-and-squirrels game: 'It is the *only* level on which Jimmy and Alison's marriage really works' (Trussler, 1969: 45). In contrast to many previous accounts, which over-emphasized the political aspects of the play and its author's role as a spokesman for his generation, Trussler stresses the personal side of Osborne's characterizations. He finds a text rich in ambiguities and meanings, reclaims it as a piece of dramatic literature, and concludes that *Look Back in Anger* is 'a well-made problem play of considerable psychological insight' (Trussler, 1969: 54). By contrast, Ronald Hayman criticized Osborne precisely for his lack of commitment to social causes. Admittedly, Jimmy makes a number of speeches on social and political subjects, but Osborne 'hasn't written a play which is committed to Jimmy's opinions' (Hayman, 1969: 22). Aesthetically, Hayman also reiterates the common criticism that *Look Back in Anger* is a 'one-man play': 'what we're given is monologue with interruption or monologue with echo' (Hayman, 1969: 17). This is more evident in reading than in production. Finally, although Martin Banham had little to add to what had previously been said, he did re-iterate the centrality of the concept of 'feeling' to Osborne's stagecraft: as texts, his plays 'do not have the logical literary quality that was Shaw's revolutionary contribution to the British theatre', but on the stage 'Osborne's plays become splendidly alive and forceful'. Unassailably, 'It is Osborne's great theatricality that most endears him and his work to actors and directors' (Banham, 1969: 2–3).

In the 1970s, the advent of feminism sharpened the critical tools at the disposal of most commentators, and suggested more acute psychological insights. In a book originally called *Look Back in Gender*, Michelene Wandor, for example, argues that Osborne's play – despite being called a 'kitchen-sink drama' – is not a 'narrative built round the woman one might expect to see working at it' (Wandor, 2001: 41). In fact, Osborne's play emphasizes Jimmy's role as a man and Alison's role as his possession, working while he sits around, ironing his shirts and even wearing one of them. Jimmy's 'battle' with Alison, argues Wandor, is as much about gender as about class. It is 'a fight for sexual identity, for it is through her that Jimmy has the potential to feel like a "real" man'. And in order to 'establish his manhood, he has to attack women' (Wandor, 2001: 43). The result is what Mary Luckhurst calls the 'centrality of misogyny' in the play (Luckhurst, 2006: 1). Misogyny is a hatred of women which is expressed both as a fear of the female – such as Jimmy's idea of Alison's sexuality as having 'the passion of a Python. She just devours me whole every time' (36) – and as a male desire to dominate women. In this view, not only is Osborne clearly misogynist, but he stages the confrontation between Jimmy and Alison in terms which emphasize her biological vulnerability. Jimmy complains that Alison doesn't feel, and his example of what he'd like to happen to her, to wake her out of her 'beauty sleep' (36), is for her to conceive a child and then miscarry. In Wandor's interpretation, Jimmy is afraid of Alison's capacity for motherhood, wishes her to suffer rather than enjoy pregnancy and is satisfied when she cannot have any more children after her miscarriage:

The play ends with Alison comforting Jimmy, her arms around him. From now on, any maternal qualities she has are for him alone. It is as if he has had to destroy (and certainly glory in the destruction of) the possibility of motherhood in her in order to gain her as a mother for himself. (Wandor, 2001: 46)

In Luckhurst's words, 'The central drama of the play is psychologically structured around the hatred of the male for the female and it's expressed in clearly misogynistic terms' (Luckhurst, 2006: 1). The obvious example is the way that Jimmy's central speech about 'good, brave causes' is bookended by two typically hostile and paranoid comments about women (89). These images of blood and butchery both play to an idea of the female as rooted in the body – women as vampires, women as bleeders – and subconsciously suggest a physical attack on women. Moreover, Osborne makes sure that Jimmy wins: at the end of *Look Back in Anger*, Alison really does suffer a miscarriage and comes back to Jimmy, proud of having suffered. Typically, his reaction to her irreducibly female misfortune is self-centred: 'It was my child too, you know. But (*he shrugs*) it isn't my first loss' (98). His selfishness is a tactic of domination. In fact, in Osborne's imagination, Jimmy's anger is constantly related to sexuality – in one passage, he states: 'Anyone who's never watched somebody die is suffering from a pretty bad case of virginity' (58). But as well as these gynaecological aspects of the text, Osborne's misogyny is expressed in the way that Jimmy is persistently feminized in his impotence. 'That a play which is seen as central to twentieth-century British theatre has a misogynist at its centre (and one who is among the great anti-heroes of British culture) says something deeply disturbing and profoundly conservative about this nation' (Luckhurst, 2006: 1). In a recent study, Luc Gilleman concludes that: 'A play that started by calling for a celebration of life in the end stands revealed not just as a humble acceptance of the complexity of existence but as a ritual exorcism of female fertility and motherhood' (Gilleman, 2002: 60).

As time has passed, feminist interpretations have lost none of their force, but the focus of interest has shifted. In 1992, Christopher Innes's standard work on post-war British drama offered a summary of *Look Back in Anger*. It 'had an impact out of all proportion to its dramatic quality. More than any other single work in the century, it was a sociological phenomenon'. At the same time, Innes analyses how 'the movement in the play is one of progressive isolation, with the protagonist driving each of his companions away' (Innes, 1992: 98) and ending up 'in a sterile and regressive childhood fantasy' (Innes, 1992: 99). The key point, however, is that Jimmy's outpourings established a new definition of authenticity of feeling on the stage, thus making the tone of previous masters such as Rattigan and Coward seem suddenly old-fashioned. It was also this sense of the authentic that was central to the criticism of Establishment values, which only offered empty wartime ideals. But although Jimmy was often identified with Osborne himself, Innes stresses the fact that the character is consciously presented 'with ambiguous irony' (Innes, 1992: 99). Nor does he ignore the play's symbolic structure, in which sex equals status: honest male proles are set against duplicitous female gentry. But the overall movement of the play is also circular, as the opening of Act Three mirrors Act One. In Alison's words, 'Jimmy is hurt because everything is the same [. . .] something's gone wrong' (70). In contrast to those responses that see the play as a radical political text, Innes argues that the dramatic statement it makes 'is bleak: there is no possibility of meaningful social change – no child of the future – and idealism equals self-destructive fantasy' (Innes, 1992: 102).

The wider social and aesthetic context of *Look Back in Anger* has been most persuasively explored in the 1990s in two books. In 1995, Stephen Lacey's *British Realist Theatre* reaffirmed 'the centrality' of the play 'as the defining theatrical event' which 'privileges a complex understanding of realism', the dominant aesthetic criterion of British culture (Lacey, 1995: 3). Exploring the complexities of the play as an event (including film versions), Lacey shows how the late 1950s and early 1960s witnessed a radical change in the way British people saw themselves and their world. Then, in 1999, Dan Rebellato's *1956 and All That* critically examined the myth of *Look Back in Anger* as an overnight revolution in British theatre, and used poststructuralist theory to re-evaluate some of the other aspects of theatre at the time. For example, he challenges the facile idea that this was simply a revolution in British culture, and uses Foucault's theory of 'the repressive hypothesis' (Rebellato, 1999: 6) to illuminate the remembered impact of Osborne's play. In *The History of Sexuality*, Foucault argued that while most people believe that the Victorians repressed all discussion of sexuality, in actual fact all social relations were actively sexualized in that era. By analogy, Rebellato argues that the way we habitually talk about *Look Back in Anger* is that it was a revolution or movement 'which had been silenced until it finally burst out at the Royal Court Theatre'. This 'image of repression' serves to legitimize not an idea waiting to break through, but rather the 'production of a new [idea]' (Rebellato, 1999: 6). It should be noted that Foucault's theory is about how we think about the past, and although some of its aspects have been refuted by detailed historical research, its critical force remains strong. When applied to 1956, it illuminates in a revealing way a common-sense habit of mind that often distorts the past. In other words, using Foucault in this instance gives you an insight that you might not otherwise have had. By looking carefully at the text of *Look Back in Anger*, Rebellato also teases out some of the suppressed sexual ambiguity of the play. Jimmy's costume for the first production – which Rebellato illustrates with a production photograph showing Alec McCowan in the recast version (Rebellato, 1999: 220–1) – recalls the underground '"Clone" look' of gays in the 1950s. In fact, the character Webster seems to embody a parallel Jimmy, someone who also feels passionately and has a cause. Osborne, argues Rebellato, wants to give Jimmy a masculine sensibility, but because of his aggression towards women, it is a sensibility that hovers around the homoerotic (Rebellato, 1999: 219–21). In the end, Jimmy has to distinguish himself from Webster because, after all, he is not homosexual. Rebellato's subtle readings of the play in its social and theatrical context succeed in his mission 'to make the familiar unfamiliar' (Rebellato, 1999: 226).

Another important revisionist reading of *Look Back in Anger*, also published in 1999, was that of Dominic Shellard in his *British Theatre Since the War*. He points out that 'although it is customary to describe *Look Back in Anger* as the first dramatic phenomenon to become a media event, this description more accurately belongs to *Waiting for Godot*' (Shellard, 1999: 47). Shellard's reading of the original production of Osborne's play stresses the fact that, at the time, it was shocking as a performance: 'One contemporary witness, Bernice Coupe, remembered that the first shock of the evening was the depressing nature of the Porters' flat, and she was particularly disconcerted by the sight of the ironing-board'. As well as describing such sights, Shellard stresses the significance of the unfamiliar sound of Jimmy's voice: 'the unmellifluous rasp of the accusations' (Shellard, 1999: 52). But although he acknowledges the importance of the play as a media event and as an articulation of an awakened liberal conscience, Shellard also offers a reassessment by quoting Jack Reading, vice-president of the Society for Theatre Research, who witnessed the debuts not only of Osborne and Beckett, but of Shelagh Delaney as well. At the time, he says, *Waiting for Godot* was more impressive in terms of form and content than *Look Back in Anger*. He then makes a case for *A Taste of Honey* (Theatre Royal Stratford East, 1958) being 'overlooked as an example of new theatre in advance of its time' (Shellard, 1999: 70).

In 2001, Peter Buse attempted a psychological reading of *Look Back in Anger* by using the concept of desire theorized by French psychologist Jacques Lacan in his essay, 'The Signification of the Phallus', which was first published in 1958. Buse shows how Jimmy's 'petulant demands' for newspapers, food, drink and attention exemplify 'precisely the Lacanian lesson about desire: it is perverse and restless' (Buse, 2001: 15). Thus Jimmy's longing for 'a little ordinary human enthusiasm' (8) is interpreted as a Lacanian 'big Other', while the apparent contradiction between his insistent desire for love and his constant dismissal of love are also consistent with Lacanian theory. The play's ending, in which Jimmy ends up with Alison, who is unable to give him what he wants, and loses Helena, who might, is interpreted thus: 'Here is desire in all its perversity – it is not really interested in getting what it wants, but is instead obsessed by the lack or loss which propels it' (Buse, 2001: 19). In this context, the bears-and-squirrels game is 'an attempt to exit the symbolic order [of language] for a while and find satisfaction at an imaginary level' (Buse, 2001: 21). According to Buse, the sexism of the play lies in the fact that while Jimmy's desire is shown as infinitely unsatisfied and unsatisfiable, the women's desire is finite: Alison and Helena 'differ from Jimmy in being able to speak or name their desire' (Buse, 2001: 19). Finally, the achievement of the play is that it manages, and in the best Lacanian tradition, to keep 'the objects of desire at a distance', that is, offstage or in a nostalgic past (Buse, 2001: 25).

It is a powerful testament to the importance of _Look Back in Anger_ that the meaning of the play remains as controversial among theatre practitioners as among academic commentators. Of course, Osborne himself had no patience with theories about his play. In his 'Author's Note' to _Déjà vu_, his 1992 sequel to _Look Back in Anger_, he states: 'Wearisome theories about J. P.'s sadism, anti-feminism, even closet homosexuality are still peddled to gullible students by dubious and partisan "academics"'. Having said that, he has his own theory: 'J. P. is a comic character. He generates energy but, also, like, say, Malvolio or Falstaff, an inescapable melancholy' (Osborne, 1996b: 279–80).

By contrast, playwright David Edgar situates Jimmy and *Look Back in Anger* firmly in the cultural politics of the 1950s. The new wave of Kitchen-Sink Drama, he persuasively argues, attacked not only the genteel drawing-room plays of Rattigan and Coward, but also had two other targets: 'the culture from which most of them [the playwrights] had escaped: John Osborne bitterly resented the narrow, lower-middle-class culture he'd left behind. Another [target] was the mass popular culture beginning to be imported from America' (Edgar, 1999: 6). Edgar sees the main theme of the first New Wave as welfare state Britain and says that it asked the highly political question: 'how the working class would use its new-found wealth and power'. He also notes a failure of nerve at the heart of Osborne's play, joking that at the end of the 'good, brave causes' speech, Cliff is handed (by Helena) 'not a revolution-ary placard or manifesto but a clean shirt' (Edgar, 1999: 9). The metaphor is apt: despite his rhetoric, Jimmy is trapped in domestic politics. Finally, Edgar reasserts the centrality of Osborne's play to the great tradition of British new writing for the theatre by pointing out that 1990s playwrights such as Mark Ravenhill are the contemporary heirs to the first new wave: 'Ravenhill has more in common with Osborne than with Coward' (Gibbons, 1999).

Ravenhill himself has a slightly different view. In a widely quoted 1999 newspaper article, Ravenhill argued that the new wave playwrights of the 1950s, led by Osborne, were 'straight boys' whose mission it was to clear away the 'feyness and falseness' of post-war theatre dominated by gay writers such as Rattigan and Coward (Gibbons, 1999; see also Edgar, 1999: 48–51). However unconscious this move was, the results were a reassertion of straight ideas of masculinity. Instead of the class terms in which the moment of 1956 is usually discussed, Ravenhill – in a clear echo of Rebellato's book – outlines the suppressed sexual politics of the New Wave. He sees the clash as that between an effete gay Establishment and the vigorous, straight new arrivals. Certainly

Ravenhill has a point: Osborne did go to some lengths to stress his heterosexuality, and although in 1959 he defended homosexuals against tabloid hysteria in the *Daily Express*, he simultaneously attacked 'narcissistic' '"Queers" theatre' (De Jongh, 1992: 108). But Osborne's relationship with gays was ambiguous. In the 1950s, his best friend, Anthony Creighton, was gay, and so was his friend 'from rep days', director John Dexter, 'the model' for Webster (Wardle, 1978: 193). Although Ravenhill's claims have been dismissed by Osborne's official biographer (Heilpern, 2006: 188–90), it is true that Osborne did make homophobic statements, although most of them come from the later, curmudgeonly, part of his career. Osborne's 'ambivalent and sometimes irrational attitude to homosexuals' (De Jongh, 1992: 108) is clearly problematic, and Ravenhill's comments did bring to public attention an aspect of theatre history which had been under-publicized.

His intervention also suggests, and this is surely confirmed by the plethora of articles, events and discussions that emerged in 2006 during the fiftieth anniversary of the play's premiere, that *Look Back in Anger* remains a play that is full of meaning, and that its significance remains hotly contested to this day.

show that, despite the fact that this play was later seen as the har-binger of Kitchen-Sink Drama, there is no kitchen sink. But, since the room is an attic, there is a cistern at the front of the stage. If the play's laddishness is emphasized by a box which bears the legend 'BEER IS BEST', its politics of disillusionment is neatly conveyed by a newspaper poster about rising prices which is pinned to the wall: UP AGAIN: BREAD PHONES SMOKES. In this produc-tion, music was also important: 'Each curtain went up with dead-beat traditional jazz with plenty of trumpet' and 'at the end of the first scene in Act Two, Bunk Johnson's "Just a closer walk with thee" was brought in, harsh and loud' (Osborne, 1957: n. pag.). Other mood music included Vaughan Williams's Symphony in E. Actors Kenneth Haigh (Jimmy), Mary Ure (Alison) and Alan Bates (Cliff) performed the play, which – on the Lord Chamberlain's insistence – had nine changes, including 'the cutting of a "lavatory" and a "homosexual" reference and the alteration of a phrase that contained the words "excessive love-making"' (De Jongh, 2000: 182). Haigh's style emphasized Jimmy's declamatory rudeness, his rhetorical hectoring and his deliberate antagonism, while Ure went on ironing 'with a look of blanched sorrow on her face, which is white and exhausted after a hundred sleepless nights, tormented by a hundred ceaseless headaches' (Hobson, 1984: 190). The acting was probably quite raw, and some witnesses remembered unforget-table 'moments of naked emotion', such as 'Haigh's breathless, feverish incredulity when Jimmy Porter returned from the funeral to find that Alison had just walked out on him' (Hayman, 1969: 90). Osborne remembers one drawback of this casting: whenever Haigh 'wasn't feeling it', he would miss out a speech (Osborne, 1991: 57). So not every performance was exactly the same.

Legendary first nights tend to divide opinion. The actual experi-ence of 8 May 1956 was, despite its historical significance, probably quite low key. Both Osborne and Tony Richardson, his director, agree that it was undramatic. Richardson said,

I remember terribly vividly the next day with John Osborne sitting in a little coffee bar down the road from the Court and we were reading the notices and generally commiserating and coffee was all we could afford in those days. And I just thought what a very depressing and flat experience the whole thing had been. (Palmer, 2006)

For Osborne, 'It just seemed a rather dull disappointing evening. But I mean people tell me they sat there rigid with excitement – I don't know, if they did, they certainly didn't exhibit it' (Palmer, 2006). By contrast, *Observer* critic Kenneth Tynan insisted that he was instantly excited by Jimmy:

One began to respond within ten minutes to this blazing figure on stage who was spraying out all the ideas and thoughts one had half-articulated in the previous ten years. One began to hear splendid grunts around one; the grunts of the affronted began to be heard. Grumbles, and then I think in the second half I heard a few seats clang and I heard the exit door go bang a couple of times. (Palmer, 2006)

The evening was 'a slap in the face' of the Establishment (Palmer, 2006). Tynan's fellow critic, and rival, Harold Hobson of the *Sunday Times*, was sceptical:

The first performance did have an emotional effect on one person in the audience, but that nobody who was there with him guessed this until the following Sunday. I refer to Kenneth Tynan. Tynan's breast was torn with passion and emotion. The play he regarded as a tremendous political statement. Otherwise the first night was entirely unmemorable. (Palmer, 2006)

Theatre productions live on in the memory, and no doubt Tynan convinced himself that the first night was more dramatic than it had been – but that is the nature of memory.

Most accounts of 8 May 1956 agree that Hugh Binkie Beaumont, king of the West End commercial producers, walked out at the interval, and that Terence Rattigan would have followed suit if he hadn't been dissuaded by T. C. Worsley, critic of the *New Statesman*. When Rattigan left at the end he told John Barber of the *Daily Express*: 'I think the writer is trying to say: "Look, Ma, how unlike Terence Rattigan I'm being."' When this remark appeared in the newspaper, Rattigan wrote to George Devine to apologize, claiming that all he meant was that 'I felt occasionally the author was being a little self-conscious about his "modernism"' (Roberts, 1999: 48).

Despite the legend that most critics hated the show, many of them welcomed Osborne as a new talent, even when they deplored the tone and content of his play. The opening line of *The Times* review was typical: 'This first play has passages of good violent writing, but its total gesture is altogether inadequate.' While the *Evening Standard* and *Evening News* vigorously attacked the play, saying that 'it aims at being a despairing cry but achieves only the stature of a self-pitying snivel' and is 'the most putrid bosh', the *Daily Express* recognized it as 'young, young, young' and most reviewers saw Osborne as a promising writer (Taylor, 1968: 35–56). Review headlines included 'Youthful Shocker, But –', 'Backstreet Hamlet Talks Bosh', 'Mr Osborne Builds a Wailing Wall' and 'Mary Ure Triumphs Over Undress'. The more literal-minded critics made feeble jokes about Alison's inability to iron efficiently. On the BBC Third Programme's *The Critics*, a show presented by Sir Gerald Barry, Ivor Brown emphasized the class aspects of the play: 'It is difficult to believe that a colonel's daughter, brought up with some standards, which we are led to believe Alison is, would have stayed in this sty for a day' (Lawson,

2006). He was not the only one to make such a point. Then, in the Sunday papers, Hobson gave the play a measured welcome, while Tynan went wild: 'It is the best young play of its decade.' His review subsequently became as legendary as the play. Today, it seems stronger on rhetoric – 'I doubt if I could love anyone who did not wish to see *Look Back in Anger*' – than on substance (Tynan, 2007: 112–13). Still, it certainly helped turn the play into a cultural phenomenon.

Despite the controversy, *Look Back in Anger* was not an instant success. Devine had programmed four slots of four performances (starting on 8 May, 24 May, 4 June and 14 June), and then it was brought back into repertory on 26 July, and ran until 1 August. Then it played on 9–15 August and, following the withdrawal of Nigel Dennis's *Cards of Identity*, it ran for nine and a half weeks nightly after 23 August. So the production history of the original version of the play is quite complicated. One fact is certain: it limped along in box office terms. 'The five-shilling seats were sold, but the percentage of financial capacity was very low indeed' (Browne, 1975: 21). Some potential audience members may have been confused by the system of running new plays in repertory, but press releases stressing the Angry Young Man angle did help boost attendance (Browne, 1975: 25).

Audiences had mixed reactions: William Gaskill, a young actor who later become a director and then head of the Royal Court in 1965, was a friend of Richardson's. He found in the play a 'passion and freshness, a rhetoric that had gone from theatre: one person speaking directly to the audience' (Lawson, 2006). At other performances, some audience members talked back: 'They used to stand up and shout and say: "I'm taking my wife out of the theatre", and all that sort of thing. "Take that horrible man off." And "Why don't you hit him back",' remembered Osborne (Palmer, 2006). Others confirm that demonstrative, noisy walkouts were frequent. As usual, this merely underlined the play's contemporaneity. It also testified to its power to dismay and annoy, characteristics which were by no means confined to its opening run. When it toured to Torquay, one member of the public complained that it was the 'outpouring of a cesspool mind' (De Jongh, 2000: 176). But if Jimmy had working-class origins, his audiences did not: 'The ordinary working man was just as likely to want to take a strap to Jimmy Porter as any retired Brigadier was; the new audience was a small, lower middle-class intelligensia whose frustrations and bayings were reflected in the play' (Watt, 1965: 59). One of the many young people who saw the original production, Derek Smith (a 29-year-old London County Council clerk who later became an RSC actor) remembers: 'Kenneth Haigh was a rather attractive figure. Clean-cut, young, dynamic. He was saying all these outrageous things, attacking the Establishment, but that actually meant something to me' (Interview). Another, Jacqueline Glasser (a 19-year-old secretary who became a literary agent) says, 'I must have read about *Look Back in Anger* because I used to get *Plays and Players* since I was 15. I remember arguing with my father and saying that Rattigan was so old-fashioned and that Osborne was incredibly fresh and new, and had a different view of the world. I felt Alison was a victim. I think that she came out of that background where you just buttoned your lip. She knew that if she answered back she'd just be asking for more. I didn't like the way Alison was treated, but I felt that she should learn to stand up for herself' (Interview).

Help for the play's box office came from the new medium of television. Osborne was interviewed on *Panorama* on 9 July, and then came the turning point. Richardson remembers that he set up a three-week transfer to the Lyric, Hammersmith, and 'I did a TV version of Act 2 [Scene Two] that generated enough interest to sell out those three weeks [which started on 5 November]. On later revivals we did OK but not sensational business' (Richardson, 1993: 79). The Lyric, Hammersmith production featured Richard

Pasco as Jimmy, Doreen Aris as Alison and Alan Bates as Cliff. Richardson's 18-minute extract, introduced by Lord Harewood (the Queen's cousin and member of the Royal Court board), was shown on BBC television on 16 October 1956, reaching an audience of about five million. Box office takings went up from £900 to £1,700, remembered Osborne (1991: 23). According to Lindsay Anderson, this was 'largely a young public' (Anderson, 1957: 164). On Wednesday 28 November the play – in a 'full' 90-minute version starring Pasco and Bates as Jimmy and Cliff – was broadcast at peak viewing time by Granada, the commercial station (Fowler, 2005: 45). On 25 February 1957, the production went on a long nationwide tour, starting at the Arts Theatre, Cambridge, while the London production was revived with Pasco, Bates and Heather Sears on 11 March 1957. By the end of that month, Royal Court accounts show that the play had by far the most performances of any of the repertoire, 151, more than double the 60 of *The Country Wife*. It had sold some 67.8 per cent of seats and brought in box office takings of £23,089 (Browne, 1975: 112). Alec McCowen played Jimmy and Clare Austin Alison at the Royal Court in November 1957, and the play clocked up 104 performances in 1957–8 (Browne, 1975: 113). Other actors who played Jimmy include Alan Dobie, and other Alisons were Tarn Bassett and Pamela Thomas. But although producer Donald Albery offered *Look Back in Anger* to the West End if Osborne cut the bears-and-squirrels ending, Osborne refused and the idea of a transfer evaporated. Meanwhile, other theatres began to get interested.

In 1957, the Bristol Old Vic Company staged an Arts-Council-funded *Look Back in Anger* at the Theatre Royal, Bristol. Directed by John Moody and starring Peter O'Toole as Jimmy and Wendy Williams as Alison, it opened on Easter Monday, 22 April, and ran for three weeks. O'Toole's Jimmy occasionally overstepped the mark: Williams remembers that, at the dress rehearsal, he suddenly threw a cup at her. A model of the Bristol Old Vic set, by Patrick Robertson, was on display at London's Theatre Museum and it shows a similar bed, arm chairs and cistern to that of the London production. Anthony Hopkins, a music student at the time, saw this production and decided to become an actor. Later, Williams toured to the Moscow Arts Theatre for the city's Youth Festival with the Royal Court production of the play in August 1957. Although Richardson said that 'people fought for tickets' (Richardson, 1993: 92), performances were partly inaudible as people who knew English translated the play for their friends while it was being performed. Another production ran for a week in Zurich and another in Sweden. In Britain, the play gradually became a repertory favourite, with some 25 local productions starring young actors such as O'Toole, Ian Holm, Derek Jacoby, Harold Pinter, Sheila Hancock and Vanessa Redgrave. These local productions meant that *Look Back in Anger* was not just a metropolitan phenomenon: people all over Britain had a chance to see it – even if they'd missed the television screenings.

The New York premiere of the play opened at the Lyceum Theatre on 1 October 1957, with a cast led by Kenneth Haigh and Mary Ure. Arguably, American audiences had less trouble with the tone of the play: 'Already accustomed to the emotional fireworks of O'Neill, Williams, Miller and Odets, Americans more easily appreciated the raciness of Osborne's dialogue' (Gilleman, 2002: 46). Although initially successful, it began to falter after about four months. So Osborne's Broadway producer, David Merrick, hired a woman for $250 to jump on stage and slap Haigh's face 'on behalf of wronged women everywhere' (Heilpern, 2006: 203). Or so the story goes. The play ran for 15 months.

First film version

The New Wave in British theatre begun by *Look Back in Anger* was also taken up by the British film industry. In the late 1950s and early 1960s, a rash of social realism in cinema was exemplified by gritty films such as *Room at the Top* (1959), *Saturday Night and Sunday Morning* (1960), *A Kind of Loving* (1962), *The Loneliness of the Long Distance Runner* (1962) and *This Sporting Life* (1963). Although these films were based on successful novels, often by writers who were seen as Angry Young Men – such as Alan Sillitoe and John Braine – others were based on successful stage plays, notably *A Taste of Honey* (1961) and *Billy Liar* (1963). Once again, the pioneering film was 1959's *Look Back in Anger*, directed by Richardson and starring Richard Burton, Mary Ure and Claire Bloom. It was produced by Woodfall Films, which had been set up by Richardson and Osborne to produce the latter's plays. Osborne's follow-up, *The Entertainer*, was also filmed by the company, as were *Saturday Night and Sunday Morning* and *A Taste of Honey*. Directors such as Anderson and Richardson worked in both film and theatre; actors from Devine's English Stage Company also worked in film. Such cultural crossovers were a sign of creative confidence.

British New Wave cinema was distinguished by its commitment to gritty realism, emotional truth and breaking taboos about representing sex. As Richardson said: 'It is absolutely vital to get into British films the same sort of impact and sense of life that what you can call loosely the Angry Young Man cult has had in the theatre and literary worlds' (Hill, 1986: 40). This occurred in the context of a steep decline in cinema audiences, mostly caused by the doubling in ownership of television sets after the broadcasting of Elizabeth II's Coronation in 1953: in 1955, there were 1,082 million annual cinema visits; by 1959, this had fallen to 581 million. New Wave films offered a view of Britain that was black and white, documentary in style and outdoor in location, rather than the glossy studio pictures of the mainstream cinema, and regional rather than metropolitan. *Look Back in Anger* was not simply the film of the play, but a new creation, with a screen-play written by Nigel Kneale (although Osborne is credited with additional dialogue).

In the process of moving from stage to screen, *Look Back in Anger* is opened out in terms of space. Although many scenes take place in the Porters' claustrophobic living room, or their equally constricted corridors and landings, others take the audience to a jazz club, a doctor's surgery, the street outside the house, the street market where Jimmy and Cliff have their stall and to Mrs Tanner's funeral. 'One of the results of this opening out of the action is that far more of the society in which the characters move is actually shown' (Lacey, 1995: 169). This, of course, contributes to both the film's documentary feel and its relevance. Some changes may have been made because of 'the desire to appeal to a young audience' (Lacey, 1995: 178). The film begins not in a room but in a club, with Jimmy joyfully playing the trumpet. In the play, Jimmy's jazz playing is a constant reminder of his presence in the flat, even when he is offstage; in the film, it suggests that rather than being alien-ated, Jimmy is cool. It aligns him with the left-liberal intelligentsia and respectable popular culture (in contrast to rock 'n' roll yobs). His audience in the club is mixed: male and female, black and white. Here, Jimmy symbolizes the three themes 'that meant most in international cinema in the 1950s – the generation gap, race prejudice and jazz music' (Walker, 1974: 61).

More crucially, the film differs from the first stage version in its portrayal of Jimmy and Cliff. Burton's Jimmy is able to roam freely over the social landscape: he has a drink with Mrs Tanner; he disrupts the Loamshire play that Helena is rehearsing; he defends Kapur, an Asian market trader; he provokes an audience member at a cinema showing an Empire war film. Burton may have been too

Victor Henry as Jimmy, Jane Asher as Alison and Martin Shaw as Cliff. This revival was a cultural cauldron, full of extraneous meanings. For the first time, because the Lord Chamberlain's office had just been abolished, the play was performed in an uncensored version. But despite the casting of 1960s pop celebrity Asher (she had been Paul McCartney's hypergamic muse since 1963), the play seemed dated. In a year which had witnessed student uprisings all over the world, *Look Back in Anger*'s politics seemed mild and old-fashioned. By chance, of course, the Royal Court's Sloane Square location was situated opposite the King's Road, which symbolized the Swinging Sixties with its Flower Power and mini-skirts. Reviews of Page's revival mention the wearing of skirts below the knee, as well as the baggy sweaters and the austerity of the set with its post-war puritan drabness and dusty Penguin paperbacks. Some thought that the play was now a dated costume drama. Certainly, Henry was less electric and more neurotic than Haigh, and Asher stronger and more stubborn than Ure. Apparently, the Strindbergian sado-masochism of their marriage came across well. In the end, this 'highly successful' production ran for 52 performances, selling 89.5 per cent of seats (Browne, 1975: 82, 124). In the West End, it opened at the Criterion Theatre on 10 December 1968.

For most of the 1970s and 1980s, *Look Back in Anger* played in many regional repertory theatres. It was a play that most local theatres put on, and that everyone saw, but which seldom enjoyed a memorable revival. In the 1970s, the gender issues of the play were explored more fully as feminism began to affect productions, and Alison emerged as a much more powerful stage presence. There were calls for a play with a central Jenny Porter figure. Meanwhile, European productions tended to cut the character of the colonel and seek contemporary resonance by using more up-to-date costumes. More traditionally, there was a revival in New York at the Roundabout Theatre, opening on 19 June 1980, with Malcolm McDowell as Jimmy, directed by Ted Craig. In the same year, a filmed version of this production was made for PBS, directed this time by Lindsay Anderson.

A play that was increasingly accused of misogyny took a while to find a female director. In 1989, Judi Dench directed a Renaissance Theatre Company production with Kenneth Branagh as Jimmy and Emma Thompson as Alison. This started at the Grand Opera House, Belfast, 6–10 June, where it raised £50,000 for charity, then played for one night at the Coliseum, London, before opening on 7 August at the Lyric, Shaftesbury Avenue, where it ran until 2 September. Branagh's Jimmy was notable as the only one that Osborne approved of: 'he succeeded in taking the rant out of the part' (Osborne, 1996b: xii). He was certainly a quieter Jimmy than some previous interpreters of the part, and came across as both more jokey and more intense. His vaudeville routines were particularly striking. But unkind reviewers saw him as petulant rather than angry; others appreciated his quiet desperation as he tried to break down his wife's indifference. Thompson came across as a cool, watchful woman, whose genteel stoicism was a form of passive resistance. On 9 August, the press night was disrupted when an angry young woman walked out in Act One, calling the production 'dreadful', the 'worst' she'd ever seen. By chance, Branagh was able to respond with Jimmy's line about 'the eternal flaming racket of the female' (20). Time had certainly not cooled the play's sexual politics. Later on, Dench 'agreed that "he [Branagh] wasn't the bastard that perhaps Jimmy Porter should have been. Porter should be more ruthless, and Kenny is not ruthless"' (Shuttleworth, 1995: 230). Later in the run, on 20 August, Branagh and Thompson married, attracting publicity as a celebrity couple. Their production was filmed for television, with David Jones directing, and broadcast in August. Starting like a pastiche of *Coronation Street*, this version captures some of Branagh's onstage playfulness – such as his pronunciation of Jimmy's 'declare herself for love' (7) as an ironic 'lurve' – and its ending movingly conveys Alison's abasement, and the couple's exhaustion.

Déjà vu and after

In 1992, Osborne's *Déjà vu*, which revisits the characters of *Look Back in Anger* almost 40 years on, arrived at the Comedy Theatre in the West End after opening (like the original production) on 8 May, this time at the Thorndike Theatre, Leatherhead. It was directed by Tony Palmer, and starred Peter Egan as J. P. (Jimmy Porter). Critics compared this old J. P. unfavourably to his younger incarnation, Jimmy, and scorned Osborne's desire to attack what he saw as politically correct targets: a 'black feminist dike', a 'native of Wogga Wogga', 'young gays' or vergers wearing 'ladies' under-clothes' (Osborne, 1996b: 297, 302, 341, 343). This was seen as tediously and mindlessly aggressive. Still, the play proved that, even at his worst, Osborne retained an instantly recognizable voice which felt passionate even when it was outdated.

However, the most important production of *Look Back in Anger* during the 1990s was that of director Gregory Hersov, and he did two versions, both with Michael Sheen. Sheen first played the role at the Royal Exchange, Manchester, with Claire Skinner as Alison in a production which ran from 26 January to 25 February 1995. The theatre is in the round, so – depending on where they were sitting – audience members might have a stronger kinship to either Jimmy, whose armchair was on one side of the stage or Alison, whose ironing board and bed represented her territory. The politics of space came across clearly, and when the characters sat down to eat together in the middle of the stage, it was a powerful image of reconciliation, however temporary. Sheen, fresh from playing Lord Fancourt Babberley in Brandon Thomas's *Charley's Aunt* (Royal Exchange, 1994–5), came on with a trumpet and blew some notes as the background glowed blue then red, followed by a bebop track. As the rest of the cast walked on, it felt as if combat had started. All of Jimmy's yearning was brought out when Sheen leant over the ironing board to deliver the 'good, brave causes' speech. By moving into Alison's world, he revealed his vulnerability. Reviews testify to the production's blazing mix of pain and passion. The *Observer*'s Michael Coveney saw Sheen's Jimmy 'as a witty, existentialist motormouth hovering between Hamlet and Mike Leigh's Johnny in *Naked*, a confused and pathetic creature whose political hatreds and anxieties are inseparable from noisy, unattractive displays of a flawed virility. Sheen is fast and mercurial, eaten with dismay and frustration, not merely angry' (5 February 1995).

Since Osborne had died just a month before, the production had the slight air of a memorial, with his widow, Helen Osborne, praising Hersov's version. The other cultural phenomenon that inflected the play's meaning was the popularity of Brit Pop, as Oasis revived memories of Jimmy Porter with their song, 'Don't Look Back in Anger'. Hersov remembers that Sheen had to struggle nightly to win over the Manchester hard men in the audience. There were also different generational reactions: older people remembered the impact of the original, while youth compared Jimmy with Liam Gallagher. Hersov also says that, when auditioning, all the actors in their mid-20s said the same thing: they hated the play as teenagers, but loved it as they got older. Their experiences of living in their own flats had caught up with the play. It made more sense as they got older. And, in rehearsals, he noticed that whenever he talked about the savagery of love, the cast would always lean forward.

Hersov's production was revived, almost five years later, at the National Theatre, running in repertory from 15 July to 11 September 1999. At the National, Hersov changed the trumpet opening, because it was a bit too bombastic, so the play began more quietly. On a cluttered set whose armchairs and ironing board were dwarfed by a huge roof, the red glow of the play's opening signalled the furnace of emotional conflict to come. Instead of the usual two intervals, he put one interval just after Alison goes to church. This decision stressed the love story aspect of the play, and ended the first half on Jimmy's defeat. As Sheen collapsed, red light bathed the stage. Being more experienced than when he first tackled the role, Sheen explored it more. He started off by playing it at a tremendous pace, and then as the run went on he tended to find spaces in which he could slow down and dig deeper into the scene, especially the silences. The scene when Jimmy and Cliff talk about Cliff leaving was played differently every night. And the play ended with Emma Fielding's Alison raining blows on Sheen's head. Fielding certainly brought a more defiant edge to the part. The *Financial Times*'s Alastair Macaulay wrote that she catches 'the implacable passive aggression behind the ironing board, the whimsical tenderness, and finally the gut-wrenched misery and need' (19 July 1999).

Regional productions of *Look Back in Anger* were by now a regular occurrence. A Glasgow Citizens production, directed by Kenny Miller, played in November 1995, with Paul Albertson as a skinhead Jimmy. His accent was reminiscent of Gazza (footballer Paul Gascoigne) and he sucked on a joint to ambient dance music rather than puffing on a pipe to jazz. In March 2001, a Bristol Old Vic production, directed by Gareth Machin, starred Nick Moran, famous after appearing in the 1998 British gangster movie *Lock, Stock and Two Smoking Barrels*. Reviews commented on the significance of Moran's casting and on his dreary, nasal, London whine. This time, the ironing board was positioned centre stage, and more than one critic felt that Helen Franklin's Alison got the better of Moran's Jimmy.

In January–February 2005, there was an important revival of the play at the Lyceum Theatre in Edinburgh, which transferred to the Theatre Royal Bath. Directed by Richard Baron, David Tennant played Jimmy and Kelly Reilly Alison. *Guardian* critic Mark Fisher reported:

> Tennant perches on the furniture, juts out his lower jaw, lobs around teapots, newspapers and food, gleefully exposing Porter's misogyny and insensitivity, even as he turns on the charm to show the charismatic lover or the vulnerable child beneath. It's a tremendous performance, given touching and credible support from the rest of the cast and finally revealing, behind the strangeness and vitriol, a sweetly conventional love story. (19 January 2005)

Tennant, who wore a dressing gown or sometimes a T-shirt, was perfectly matched by Reilly's Alison, who had a hypnotic grace both subtle and plaintive, as well as an ability to smoulder dangerously.

As part of the Royal Court's 50th anniversary celebrations of the start of the English Stage Company, and the premiere of *Look Back in Anger*, a radio version was broadcast on BBC Radio 4 on 1 April 2006. Ben Whishaw played Jimmy and Samantha Young Alison in this 90-minute adaptation, directed by Lu Kemp. Ben Whishaw's mockney accent was youthful but also monotonous, and irritatingly self-righteous rather than compellingly angry. Oddly enough, the most moving moment was when a lone trumpet played the National Anthem at the end of the play. Perhaps the trouble with film or radio adaptations of *Look Back in Anger* is that there is no direct relationship between Jimmy and the audience – and this rapport is the essence of the play's passionate intensity.

The only stage revival to celebrate *Look Back in Anger*'s 50th anniversary was directed by Royal Court veteran Peter Gill at the Theatre Royal, Bath. Running between 16 August and 2 September, it featured Richard Coyle as Jimmy, Mary Stockley as Alison and Rachael Stirling as Helena. William Dudley's set was claustrophobic, with the cistern at roof level, weighing down on the occupants. Coyle's Jimmy was a vulnerable northerner, and his favourite pose was striding around with his hands in his pockets. Notable was the soundscape which used jazz music to emphasize key moments, such as Jimmy's attack on Alison's brother Nigel, or the distant sounds of war when he talked about the Spanish Civil War or a bugle during Colonel Redfern's account of leaving India. There was a real sense of shock as Jimmy hurried Helena to bed before the curtain fell for one interval. Reviews were moderate and not enough to support a West End transfer.

But while most productions of *Look Back in Anger* have a contemporary resonance, some are more resonant than others. A good example of the tension between the 1950s and the 2000s could be seen in Pilot Theatre Company's 2007 touring production, which mixed a set design that was influenced by the Vorticist art movement with a cast that reflected contemporary Britain rather than the Britain of Empire days. Cliff was played by Iranian actor Davood Ghadami (Tariq in Pilot's *East Is East*) and Helena by Rina Mahoney (often seen playing Asian characters in television soaps). Director Marcus Romer saw the play as having especial interest to a multi-ethnic audience brought up on reality TV, and familiar with programmes such as *Coronation Street*, *Shameless* and *Skins*. In his production, some lines sounded suddenly fresh: Jimmy's 'Did you ever see some dirty old Arab' (19) or 'My mother was all for being associated with minorities, provided they were the smart, fashionable ones' (58). Romer also thought that the idea of a world where the newspapers don't tell you the truth, and where the promise of a political dawn has been overshadowed by a crisis in the Middle East, would be perfectly comprehensible to school audiences in the wake of the war in Iraq. He favoured an acting style that was intimate and suggested to audiences that they were eavesdropping on a soap opera. Certainly, his addition of the politics of ethnicity to the already highly charged sexual politics of the piece, and his view of Jimmy (played by Karl Hayes) as a serial abuser, created a production which simply would never have been possible in 1956.

4 Workshopping the Play

This chapter offers a series of practical workshop exercises based on *Look Back in Anger*. It involves discussion of the play's characters, conflicts, key scenes, motifs and ideas which a group of actors could explore practically for themselves. The content is also informed by new interviews with actors and directors who have been involved in professional productions of the play.

The world of the play

The world of *Look Back in Anger* is a fictional one. Although it bears a striking similarity to reality, and the geography of the Porters' small flat seems perfectly comprehensible to anyone living in Britain today, the world of the play is not exactly the same as real life. It is a fiction. And, in a workshop, the experience of the play from the point of view of actors is the experience of an alternative world. For most student actors, the play looks back not just to the lifetime of their parents, but to that of their grandparents and great-grandparents. So in order to explore the world of *Look Back in Anger*, it is worth distinguishing – from the very beginning – the play as it was in 1956 and the play as it is now.

Reading

Divide the playtext into sections. (Depending on the time available, this exercise could apply to the whole play, to Act One or to a smaller section.) Read each section of the text, alternating which actors play each of the characters. At the end of each section, ask two questions:

- What was old-fashioned, unfamiliar or puzzling about the text?
- What was contemporary about the text. Find and read out a line that could have been written yesterday.

Unfamiliar aspects of the text might include references to 'an air-raid warden' (4), two 'posh' Sunday papers (5) or the H-bomb (6).

Contemporary lines might include 'I just like food' (4), 'stupid bitch' (5) and 'don't be so sickening' (6).

This kind of exercise will highlight the fact that the original world of the play, that of 1956, is very distant now to most student actors. They require footnotes to understand all the cultural references. But it also underlines the fact that the play's emotional content, and much of its language, both remain thrillingly contemporary.

Visualization

As well as focusing on the word in a read-through of Act One, for example, it would also be useful to use visual aids to evoke the world of the play. Photographs of 1950s jazz musicians, politicians such as Prime Minister Anthony Eden, and ordinary street scenes evoke a black-and-white world where everything – from the posture of debutantes at an upper-class dance to the smog-filled skies of a large Midland town – seems distant. Historical.

Visualize the set: read out John Osborne's detailed stage directions at the start of the play (1–2). Show a production photograph of Alan Tagg's set for the original production of *Look Back in Anger* (e.g. Fowler, 2005: 2). What item specified by Osborne's stage directions (1) is missing on Tagg's set? (The second armchair – other production shots show that Jimmy sits on the bed while reading the newspapers.) What item is on the set that Osborne doesn't specify in the stage directions? (The cistern – why is that there and what does it mean? The cistern, especially when placed at the front of the stage, confronts the audience with the squalor of the Porters' flat. It also enables Jimmy to be very close to the audience during the 'Can you 'ear me, mother?' episode, when he plays on the cistern as if it was a pair of bongo drums (52).)

The set: then and now. Peter Gill, veteran director of the play at Theatre Royal Bath in 2006, points out that:

> What young people don't understand now is – for example – the question of where these characters would keep their clothes. These three didn't need a lot of wardrobe space: you cannot believe how little clothing people would have had in those days. Jimmy probably had two shirts, wash and wear, one pair of trousers and a mac – and that's all. (All quotations from interviews with the author unless otherwise stated.)

Gill's comments perhaps explain why Alison's suitcase is so small in the 1989 film version: she has very few possessions. Now, lead a discussion about this and the use of space, stressing the claustrophobia of three people cooped up together in the Porters' flat. As Emma Fielding, who played Alison in the 1999 National Theatre production, says, 'Remember that the play takes place in the context of a hothouse: all three of them, and then four, are living in a bedsit without much money.'

Climbing into the set: All actors to lie on the floor in comfortable positions. Each has to choose a character from the play. Remember, it's 1956. Imagine that you are a spirit and can fly in the air. Starting off in outer space, circle around the planet and then zero in, first on the British Isles, and then on a 'large Midland town' (1). Stop above the town for a moment, take in its industrial character, the factories, the railways, the churches and the market where Jimmy and Cliff have their stall. Now find the house owned by Miss Drury, the Porters' landlady, and explore the house as a floating spirit. Enter the front door. How many stairs does it have?

How are the corridors decorated? Now enter the attic flat: What is it like? What does it smell of? Colour of the surroundings? Atmosphere?

Now ask an actor to imagine themselves as one of the characters in one of the two rooms of the flat: explain what they are doing and thinking. Then act it out. Repeat as required.

Such Stanislavskian exercises help develop the feel of the characters and the sense of a lived environment, usually aiding the actors to achieve more depth and more colour in their improvisations.

The language of the play

Although some of the language of *Look Back in Anger* has dated, most of the speeches sound contemporary in their passion and directness.

Improvisation

Language: read the 'good, brave causes' speech (89) in a regional accent. First ask actors to choose an accent, then do the reading and finally discuss the changes in the meaning of the speech that result from hearing it spoken with, for example, a Yorkshire accent, a Norwegian accent or a Trinidadian accent. Next ask a student to act out the speech in the character of, for example, a Liverpudlian hairdresser, a West Country office worker or an old Jamaican man. Note the changes of meaning that differences in verbal tone and body language suggest.

In the 2006 Theatre Royal Bath production, Richard Coyle played Jimmy with a mild northern accent. He says, 'I hope I gave Jimmy an earthiness, a grounded northern quality, but also a real nastiness. One of the things I have for free is nastiness – I can play that quite easily. It comes down the bloodline – that Celtic blackness.'

In the 1999 National Theatre production, Michael Sheen used a Cockney accent. He says,

My feeling was that he was from London and he'd gone to a university, but that he remained a Londoner, hence the Cockney accent. But his accent was something he could play around with; when it suited him he would play the working-class Londoner; or he would play the university-educated middle-class guy. I tried to play around with it musically, and also because all those speeches are like jazz riffs so the accent became an added instrument in that.

Now ask the actors to read, and act out, the 'good, brave causes' speech, switching between regional accent and Received Pronunciation (RP). Does Jimmy lapse into his regional accent when he gets angry? Does he use RP when he is more reflective, or when he is showing off and making an intellectual point? Other vocal and verbal exercises could build on Osborne's suggestion that Jimmy's so-called tirades should be approached as if they were operatic 'arias' (Osborne, 1996b: 279).

Writing

Write a Jimmy Porter rant. First, in an imitation of the language and style of Osborne's original, and then in a contemporary idiom. Compare the two linguistic registers, and find out which words in the one couldn't be used in the other. Note that the stage world of 1956 was a world governed by theatre censorship, so some words, such as swear words, could not be used. A more interactive version requires members of the group to suggest topics for improvised speeches by one actor (group members can take turns).

To explore the rhythm of Osborne's writing, actors can be given a monologue and asked to rewrite it in their own chosen voice or accent. How far does the rhythm of Osborne's language survive the transposition? To explore his rhythm further, actors can punctuate a monologue with physical actions: one reads the text while another clicks their fingers for every comma, slaps their thigh for a full stop and stamps their foot for an exclamation mark.

The characters of the play

Following on from the previous visualization exercise, choose a character from the play. Imagine you are a spirit again: hover about the room where your character is alone. Give reasons for them being alone: what are they doing? What are they thinking? What are they feeling? Individual students could do an improvised monologue that explores the thoughts and feelings of their chosen character.

Then move on to exploring each main character in depth.

Group discussion

Jimmy's character. Three questions about Jimmy:

1. If he was an animal, what animal would he be?
2. What part of the body is the centre of his character?
3. What does this character want?

Obvious answers about Jimmy being a bear are less interesting than the image of him as an attack dog that needs muzzling, a boxing badger or a vulture who picks on people who are weak. Zoological fact is less relevant than the visual image: so the idea that Jimmy is a lion with a barbed penis sounds biologically unlikely but seems to fit his character.

Jimmy's centre might be his heart or his groin. His passion and aggression are central. But his fists are equally important. And maybe so are his eyes.

Jimmy's wants are best expressed in the first person: 'I want people to understand me'; 'I want to live life to the full'; 'I want respect'; 'I want proof of love'.

As Richard Baron, who directed the play at the Edinburgh Lyceum in 2005, says, 'The central theme is Jimmy's rant against inertia, his desire to be enthusiastic about life, to fully live and fully love. Despite his destructive aggression, he's also crying out for meaning in his life.' Is this Jimmy's super-objective? Discuss.

Imagine that Jimmy keeps a stash of personal items and effects in his empty trumpet case, hidden under the bed: describe some of these items and outline what they mean. If he keeps a photograph of his dad, what is the photograph of? Is it of his dad during the Spanish Civil War, or on his wedding day, or holding Jimmy when he was a baby? What can we say about Jimmy's relationship to him? How is that conveyed through a visual image? Improvise a dialogue in which Jimmy shows his precious items to Cliff, or to Helena.

With Jimmy, the question of misogyny has to be explored, despite the differing views of those who have been in productions of the play. Richard Baron says:

> Yes, misogyny is one of the accusations aimed at the play, and at Osborne himself. You have to see Jimmy in the context of his times, but you also have to acknowledge that he is very needy, wanting love, approval and attention. Osborne was also influenced by Shaw's *Man and Superman*, and Jimmy embodies the Shavian idea of women bleeding men dry. Jimmy sees domesticity as draining him of creative talent.

Emma Fielding adds:

> The common perception is that the play is hugely misogynistic, aggressive and anti-female, but much to my surprise – I must say – during the course of rehearsing it, I found something completely different: in Osborne's stage directions, it's interesting that he gives indications of what the men are feeling, but with the women he stands outside them. But I got the feeling that he rather loved women, despite what the text says.

Improvisation

Misogyny is an abstract word and what needs exploring is the feeling behind it: so improvise around the statement: 'I hate women.' Then discuss what this actually means: why do men hate women? Is it fear of being unable to satisfy them sexually? Dread of being ignored? Inability to grasp the mysteries of the female body? By contrast, improvise around the statement: 'I love my wife because . . .'

Next, first-person improvisations as Jimmy: 'I'm Jimmy and what I want is . . .' or 'I'm Jimmy and what I really hate is . . .'

Finally, in the psychiatrist's chair: an improvisation for two actors, seated opposite each other. Jimmy has gone to see a therapist. The therapist must first find out what his complaint is, and then trace it back to concrete incidents in his past. Jimmy must state why he needs help, and then reveal what he thinks are the personal origins of his present feelings.

Group discussion: Alison's character

Now repeat all the above exercises for Alison. If actors struggle to come up with imaginative choices about Alison as an animal, what does this say about her character? What are her objectives? 'I want peace'; 'I want to be safe'; 'I want to be loved.' What are the contents of her handbag? In discussions about Alison's character, watch out for the way the talk veers back towards Jimmy. If this happens, point it out. Then ask why this has happened. Is it because he dominates her, or because he dominates the play?

With Alison, the central problem might be the question of why good girls are attracted to bad boys. Wendy Williams, who played Alison at the Bristol Old Vic in 1957, says:

> People do have this rebellious nature when they're young. Parents are just old hat. I was far too suburban and sat-upon by my mother to be rebellious personally. But Alison has never been

really stretched or challenged before she meets Jimmy. And that must have been his attraction. It's exciting to meet an unsuitable boy. Much more interesting than that boring bloke your mother is so keen on. Then you can get into very deep water. Remember, in those days people didn't live together: they got married. And Jimmy has gone along with that. Not many people got divorced so Alison was trapped. And then she can't cope.

And Peter Gill adds:

> In the 1950s, posh girls dabbled with exciting but unsuitable boys. The girls were much more able to cut and run if these relationships fell apart. They came from the ruling class of the Empire so they had a good sense of their own identity.

Discuss and compare with similar scenarios today: for example, do nice girls still believe they can change bad boys?

Improvisation
Improvise a discussion between Colonel Redfern and his wife, Alison's parents, about her choice to marry Jimmy.

Emma Fielding says:

> Alison's weapon is her silence. But it's just as aggressive as Jimmy. She knows how to use her power to upset him. It was a definite decision to make her silences speak volumes. With other characters, Alison never stops talking – she's usually very vocal. Only with Jimmy does she really glower – because she knows this will hurt him.

If Alison's best weapon is her silence, improvise a scenario in which Jimmy tries to provoke her and she resists with the palm of her hand. Develop other improvisations in which silence is used as a weapon. Discuss the gender implications: is there a difference between female silence and male silence?

Now consider the view from outside: What does Miss Drury, the Porters' landlady, think about these characters? Improvise a telephone conversation, or a conversation conducted over the back-garden fence, in which Miss Drury describes the characters of her lodgers. What does she dislike about their behaviour?

The conflicts of the play

Richard Baron says, 'Although the play caught the spirit of the 1950s so well, today the most interesting thing about it is its Strindbergian aspects – the battle going on in that room, over the ironing board, is fascinating.' And Peter Gill says,

> Osborne gives voice to the neurotic or frail alpha male of the 1950s, and shows what that kind of man feels – their terrified paranoia of the duplicity of girls from the middle class. Whatever people might think about it now, this is the way that men felt in those days. It's no good judging them and saying they were bad; that's like saying Strindberg was a misogynist – so what?

The mention of Strindberg in discussions about *Look Back in Anger* is significant to understanding the play's central marital conflict. It is also worth noting that Emma Thompson, who played Alison in 1989, says that the play embodies '[Jean-Paul] Sartre's vision of hell – three people in a room' (Shuttleworth, 1995: 229).

Visualization

Visual images of marital discord (sculpting exercise): in pairs, discuss and improvise visual images of marital discord today. Then read the following passage from Kenneth Tynan's review of the play:

Mr Osborne's picture of a certain kind of modern marriage is hilariously accurate: he shows us two attractive young animals engaged in competitive martyrdom, each with its teeth sunk deep in the other's neck, and each reluctant to break the clinch for fear of bleeding to death. (Tynan, 2007: 112)

Swap pairs, and create visual images of this passage. Discuss the differences between the results of these two exercises: what is the balance of power shown? Who is the stronger: man or woman? What other images of mutual marital agony occur?

Improvisation

Improvise a scene between Jimmy and Alison, with him using verbal provocations and her using silence: such scenes usually emphasize the sheer aggression at the heart of their relationship. While Jimmy controls Alison because of his potential for physical strength, Alison controls Jimmy by means of her strong-mindedness. In the play, she is at a disadvantage because of her pregnancy. Replay the scene with this disadvantage in mind. How does this change the relationship?

Now consider the view from outside: What does Webster, the Porters' offstage gay friend, think about these characters? Improvise a monologue in which he explains what he thinks about their relationship.

Now, explore the domination of territory: Gregory Hersov, who directed the play in Manchester (1995) and London (1999), says, 'I thought the play was about four people battling for territory in a very small flat.' Emma Fielding agrees, 'Even within the room, it's all very territorial – they each have their seat or place at the ironing board.' David Tennant, who played Jimmy in Edinburgh in 2005, says:

I did quite a lot of leaping about, on the furniture, and that. A lot of bare feet and things like that. And often very few clothes as well. It felt as if we really were in this cage with all this pent-up anger and energy so it seemed natural that that would spill out into a kind of physical exuberance.

Finally, David Hare says, 'Julie Burchill describes *Look Back in Anger* as "that play where somebody does the ironing while someone else shouts at her."'

Consider these statements and explore parts of a scene with reference to the position of the characters in relation to the stage space, and in relation to each other. Does Jimmy need to climb onto the armrests of the chair in order to assert his dominance physically? Does Alison use the ironing board as a barrier, and hide behind it in a space of safety? Explore the Porters' room, dividing it into 1) personal areas; 2) neutral areas; and 3) places of danger. Discuss.

Reading

Read a scene in different regional accents, and discuss how this helps stress different aspects of the conflict between the characters. The central questions are: what do each of these characters really want? How are they trying to get it? What prevents them from succeeding?

Other relationships and conflicts that might be worth exploring are: Jimmy and Cliff (what would they argue about?); Alison and Helena (what do they have in common?); Jimmy and Helena (how is their relationship different from that of Jimmy and Alison?).

Group discussion

David Hare says:

I think the erotic charge in Osborne's writing is very important. It doesn't matter whether he was gay or not, which is rather an arid argument, but what's much more important is that he wrote in an openly sexual way. And sex is a vital part of his romanticism.

Bearing in mind Helena's surprise at the way Cliff and Alison keep embracing ('Is Cliff in love with you?', 39), what do each of the characters feel about each other?

Improvisation

Improvise a monologue each for Jimmy, Cliff and Alison in which they describe their real feelings for each other. Is Cliff secretly in love with Alison? What exactly does she feel about him?

Another good way of exploring the relationships between the characters is to take a couple of pages of Act One, and break down Jimmy's speeches into single sentences that Cliff and Alison can respond to. For example:

Jimmy	Perhaps there's a concert on.
Cliff	_____
Jimmy	(Picks up the *Radio Times*) Ah!
Alison	_____
Jimmy	(Nudges Cliff with his foot) Make some more tea.
Cliff	_____
Jimmy	Oh yes. There's a Vaughan Williams.
Alison	_____
Jimmy	Well that's something anyway. Something strong, something simple, something English.
Cliff	_____
Jimmy	I suppose people like us aren't supposed to be very patriotic.
Alison	_____
Jimmy	Somebody said it – who was it – we get our cooking from Paris (that's a laugh), our politics from Moscow, and our morals from Port Said.
Cliff	_____ (10–11)

As Michael Sheen says, 'Treat Jimmy's speeches as duologues – just because somebody doesn't have any lines it doesn't mean it isn't a duologue. Emotionally, it goes back and forth all the time.' Discuss the changes of feeling and meaning between a straight reading of this scene and the new one. Students can then compare the effect to judge the impact of Jimmy's speeches and his rhetorical flights.

At this point, it might also help to explore the subtext of some of the main speeches and conflict situations.

For example, rewrite a speech, such as Jimmy's response to the news that Cliff wants to leave, and add the subtext:

Try washing your socks. (*You stink.*) It's a funny thing. (*Listen to me.*) You've been loyal, generous and a good friend. (*Thanks, you're a mate.*) But I'm quite prepared to see you wander off, find a new home, and make out on your own. (*I don't need you anymore.*) And all because of something I want from that girl downstairs, something I know in my heart she's incapable of giving. (*Women always come between us.*) (89)

This can also be done with dialogue. Once the subtext is in place, select two actors to play Jimmy and – if, for example, it's one of the bears-and-squirrels episodes – two to play Alison. One speaks the text and the other the subtext. Sometimes this works better with the subtext spoken second, but it could also be done with the subtext spoken first. The subtext is an internal little voice, a sidekick to the character. You could try this with Jimmy's subtext being masculine or feminine, and the same gender distinctions for Alison: how does this change our view of the characters or of the conflict? What has this exercise clarified?

Note: sometimes the subtext can be non-verbal – for example, *grrrrr* (a growl of frustration).

Improvisation

The Not, but . . . (or parallel universe) exercise: Choose three key moments in the play, for example, the moment in Act One when Alison almost tells Jimmy she is pregnant (30–3); the moment at the end of Act Two when Helena slaps Jimmy's face (75–7); or the play's final scene between Jimmy and Alison (101–3). First play the scene as written, then try an improvisation in which a different outcome is sought. For example, instead of Cliff returning to interrupt Alison in Act One, she manages to tell Jimmy's she's pregnant. As Emma Fielding says, 'During the first bears-and-squirrels episode, when she's just about to tell Jimmy that she's pregnant, you can feel her deep affection and happiness.' Or what would happen if Helena didn't slap Jimmy? Or, at the end, if Jimmy didn't retreat from the truth of Alison's emotional experiences? After these improvisations, play the scene as written. How have the improvisations changed your view of the play?

Group discussion

Michael Sheen says, 'The key for me was that although Jimmy has all these huge speeches, I had to find a way in which these were all about all the other people in the room and not just about Jimmy. So each long speech was directed at one or the other of the others.' Study one or more of Jimmy's long speeches, and show how an actor can direct individual lines at each of the other people in the room. Some lines might also be introspective thoughts and others directed at the audience.

The ending – who has won?

Gregory Hersov says:

> When I first read the play, I hated the final scene, especially the stage directions: you can't do this, I thought, it's complete

rubbish. In rehearsals, what happened is that Alison began hitting Jimmy and that last speech comes out of that kind of exposed bruised thing. The play's characters slightly rebel against their creator.

Emma Fielding adds, 'Rather than being cuddled up together, we were sitting apart and facing each other: I beat him on the head with my hands. She just slaughters Jimmy. At the end, they're left on a raft of their own making.' And David Tennant says, 'With Kelly Reilly [Alison], the ending absolutely broke her heart over the loss of the baby and I think that that scares Jimmy to death. To see her vulnerability. Because he needs her to be his rock.'

Improvisation
Play the final moments of the play in different ways to illustrate different outcomes: one improvisation might involve silent tableaux of the ending. If Alison stands over Jimmy, it enhances the authority of her experience of losing her child; if Jimmy puts his head in Alison's lap, it suggests his vulnerability and a retreat into a childish world where Alison is his mother; if Jimmy ends up on the floor and Alison storms out at the end, does this change the play's meaning?

The relevance of the play

Improvisation
Recap: Ask the group to improvise a monologue in which:

1.   Cliff retells the story of Act One
2.   Helena retells the story of Act Two
3.   Alison retells the story of Act Three.

Make sure that all the significant incidents of the plot are well remembered. If any points have been forgotten, discuss the reasons for that.

Another good recapping exercise, which requires quite a lot of preparation, is for each character to speed through the play in ten minutes, speaking only a handful of key lines and exaggerating their emotions. The next stage is to choose a single verb to describe the character's state at the start of each scene and another for the end of the scene. The purpose is to clarify the character's journey through the play.

Group discussion

David Tennant says,

> Every night, the 'If you could have a child, and it would die' [36] speech got gasps. You literally had intakes of breath. The play is so well constructed that it still gets those very theatrical moments. It's hard to think of a worse statement than that speech. It reminds you that the play is not just of its historical period. The effect of that speech shows that its emotions are still powerful and relevant.

What aspects of the emotional conflict in the play remain relevant and why?

Also: Tennant continues, 'I remember that the American Age speech – "Perhaps all our children will be Americans" [11] – got a great reaction, and this idea is more current the ever now.' Discuss how the play is still relevant emotionally, as a story of three or four individuals, and how it is still relevant politically.

Improvisation

Genre: Recap the naturalistic genre of the play: to illustrate this, enact different scenes using various different genres: soap opera,

Greek tragedy, romantic comedy or Theatre of the Absurd. First discuss the characteristics of your chosen genre, the facial expressions typical of soaps or the brightness of tone of their actors, then act out the scene. Following Peter Gill's insight that 'The girls' parts are more interesting than people think. In relation to their own conversations together rather than in relation to Jimmy', you could choose the start of Act Two Scene One (37–41) between Alison and Helena. As a soap, it might be much more comic than usual: as a tragedy, some of Osborne's lines seem positively melodramatic: for example, Helena's 'Horrifying and oddly exciting' (39). You could also select a tableau, or a series of tableaux, from your chosen scene and select a contemporary pop or rock song which illustrates the emotions of the characters in the scene. Discuss.

Winding down

Having worked on *Look Back in Anger*, what image does the play bring to mind? A group of actors could act out this image (sculpting exercise).

Group discussion

What's your favourite line, and why?

Group discussion

What real-life associations does the play suggest?

It might be useful for different members of the workshop to take turns as note-takers, and to wind down at the end of each session with a physically engaging game, and a recap of work by the note-taker. Workshop leaders should also keep notes of their experiences, and perhaps encourage students by telling them of the successes of past workshops. In that way, the study of a well-known play, such as *Look Back in Anger*, can become a new adventure.

5 Conclusion

John Osborne's *Look Back in Anger* is the outstanding theatre phenomenon of British post-war culture. But while straight revivals and workshops of the play demonstrate its continued relevance, it is also possible to stage versions which deconstruct the text and reinvent it in a much more contemporary genre. For example, the innovative theatre company Frantic Assembly – which has since the early 1990s specialized in staging theatre pieces characterized by a fusion of text, dance and music – started its career by revisiting the moment of anger. Inspired by Volcano theatre company, Frantic Assembly began as a group of Swansea university graduates led by Scott Graham, Steven Hoggett and Vicki Coles/Middleton. For them, staging *Look Back in Anger* as their debut in 1994 was a strategic move:

Hoggett says,

I'd done a year with Volcano – who we all admired – after university, and before we started the company, and one of the things I'd learnt, just from being with them, was that for us to start a new company we'd need to get a nationwide tour. But we couldn't get a tour even after our Edinburgh successes unless we produced something that people had heard of. So we looked for an existing text to publicize our company. We spent a long time trying to find a text we liked or that worked. *Look Back in Anger* really was the only one we felt might work. (Interview)

Another collaborator, Spencer Hazel, 'stripped the text right back' and took out one character, Colonel Redfern. Then he developed the parallels between the two women characters, and what they represent in the play. Although it was a pared back version, it still kept Jimmy's monologues intact. 'Then it became different out of necessity: the total budget was something like £200 so the set was just a lot of ironing boards and we all wore pyjamas. It was a bit Dennis-Potterish at times, with a lot of teddy bears. The music was an impure mix of Prokofiev, Elvis Presley and Sinead O'Connor.' Frantic Assembly drew parallels between 1950s Britain and an age characterized by Douglas Coupland's novel *Generation X*. 'We started to work physically on the text,' says Hoggett, 'and that's where the company's signature style came from.'

Graham adds,

Our intention with *Look Back in Anger* was to find the guts of the play. It had become a very safe play and that seemed ludicrous to us. We knew it by reputation and we realized it had become so established, although it had once frightened people and had an effect on society. When I read it I couldn't understand how it had become so staid because emotionally it was on fire. What we wanted to do was to invent a physical language which would have some of that guts and fire about it – we wanted to contest the video culture where you can just get a classic out of the library and watch it on telly.

Frantic Assembly's situation paralleled that of the characters in *Look Back in Anger*. They were young, they had just left university, and the social and political context of the 1990s had some similarities with the complacency of the 1950s. 'Jimmy talks about "white-tile" universities and we completed our education at a time when polys were becoming unis," says Graham. 'And what does Jimmy get from further education? Nothing. He still works in a market. So

I really believed in it as a play and it felt right that our audiences should feel the play's rage. That was the effect we were looking for.'

Look Back in Anger is clearly both a well-made play and a theatre history myth. When myth and reality come into conflict, suggests *Guardian* theatre critic Michael Billington, 'The only answer, as a character says in John Ford's The Man Who Shot Liberty Valance, is "to print the legend"' (Billington, 1999). That's one way of doing it – another way would be to point out the clash between myth and reality. And versions of the play such as that which launched Frantic Assembly's career, did exactly that, by confronting an established text with an innovative theatre practice. Let us hope that more theatre-makers will make similar experiments in the future. It's a risky strategy, but a potentially exquisite one.

In his defence of John Osborne, David Hare argues that 'of all British playwrights of the twentieth century, he is the one who risked most. And, risking most, frequently offered the most rewards' (Hare, 2005: 63). Whatever its detractors say, *Look Back in Anger* has not only proved its worth on countless stages, but also proved itself in the wider world – it changed the landscape of British post-war culture. And it still does what great fiction is so good at: it not only shows us who we really are, but also suggests what we might hope to become.

Timeline 1945–60

Politics	Culture
1945 End of the Second World War; United States drops atom bombs on Hiroshima and Nagasaki in Japan; Labour wins General Election, Conservative Winston Churchill defeated and Labour leader Clement Attlee becomes prime minister	*Animal Farm* by George Orwell and *Brideshead Revisited* by Evelyn Waugh published; David Lean's film *Brief Encounter* released; as American jazz saxophonist Charlie Parker records the Savoy sessions, bebop music becomes popular
1946 National Health Service founded; Winston Churchill coins the phrase 'Iron Curtain' in an anti-Soviet speech	*An Inspector Calls* by J. B. Priestley first performed; *The Common Sense Book of Baby and Child Care* by Dr Benjamin Spock published; Council of Industrial Design's *Britain Can Make It* Exhibition displays designer household goods
1947 India and Pakistan achieve independence	French designer Christian Dior introduces the 'New Look', which defines the fashions of the post-war years
1948 In India, Mahatma Gandhi is assassinated by a Hindu fanatic; the Soviet Union stops road and rail travel between Berlin and western Germany, forcing the Western	American sexologist Alfred Kinsey publishes *Sexual Behavior in the Human Male*; English academic F. R. Leavis publishes *The Great Tradition*, an analysis of the importance of the English novel

Politics

Culture

powers to organize a massive airlift, heightening Cold War tensions

1949   Soviet Union explodes its first atomic bomb

The Cocktail Party by T. S. Eliot first performed; *A Streetcar Named Desire* by Tennessee Williams first performed in London; *Nineteen Eighty-Four* by George Orwell published; *A Writer's Notebook* by Somerset Maugham published; Carol Reed's film *The Third Man*, a Cold War thriller starring Orson Welles, released; *Death of a Salesman* by Arthur Miller opens in New York

1950   American senator Joseph McCarthy begins an anti-Communist witch-hunt

Music-hall comedian Max Miller performs his third and last Royal Command Performance at the London Palladium

1951   Conservative Party wins General Election and 77-year-old Winston Churchill becomes prime minister

Relative Values by Noël Coward first performed; film of Tennessee Williams's *A Streetcar Named Desire*, starring Marlon Brando, released; Dave Brubeck jazz quartet set up; national television broadcasting in the United States begins

1952   Britain produces its own atomic bomb; United States tests the first hydrogen bomb; George VI dies and is succeeded by his daughter Elizabeth; British colonial powers declare State of Emergency in Kenya

The Deep Blue Sea by Terence Rattigan first performed; American jazz trumpeter Dizzy Gillespie visits Paris, France

Politics

1953   Coronation of Queen Elizabeth II; Josef Stalin, Soviet leader, dies; Soviet Union tests hydrogen bomb

1954   United States tests the hydrogen bomb at Bikini Atoll, 500 times more powerful than the bomb dropped on Hiroshima; in Egypt, Colonel Gamal Abdel Nasser becomes prime minister; in Cyprus, Colonel George Grivas and EOKA (National Organisation of Cypriot Fighters) attack British troops; in Britain, wartime rationing finally stops

1955   Winston Churchill resigns as British prime minister due to ill health and is replaced by Anthony Eden

1956   Colonel Gamal Abdel Nasser elected president of Egypt; he nationalizes the Suez Canal and 'The Suez Crisis' involves the abortive invasion of the country by Israel,

Culture

The Wild One, film starring Marlon Brando, released; CBS begins its first colour television broadcasts in the United States

Lucky Jim by Kingsley Amis published; *Separate Tables* by Terence Rattigan first performed; *After the Ball* by Noël Coward first performed; *On the Waterfront* film released; *Lord of the Flies* by William Golding published; American rock 'n' roll musician Bill Haley releases 'Rock Around the Clock'; American blues singer Billie Holiday tours Europe; first portable transistor radios are marketed; Kenneth Tynan becomes theatre critic of the *Observer*

Waiting for Godot by Samuel Beckett first performed in London; commercial television introduced in Britain; Nicholas Ray's *Rebel without a Cause*, starring popular icon James Dean, released; Russian-American novelist Vladimir Nabokov publishes *Lolita*; first Disney theme park opens in California

Look Back in Anger by John Osborne first performed; *The Quare Fellow* by Brendan Behan first performed; *South Sea Bubble* by Noël Coward first performed; *The Outsider* by

Politics

Britain and France; Soviet troops suppress the popular Hungarian uprising against Communist rule; Soviet leader Nikita Khrushchev denounces Stalin's crimes in a secret speech at the Communist Party Congress

1957 Anthony Eden resigns due to ill health, and Harold Macmillan succeeds him as Conservative prime minister; Macmillan makes 'You've never had it so good' speech about increased consumer prosperity

1958 Creation of Life Peers, who sit in the House of Lords for life but could not pass on their titles; first London to Aldermaston march and birth of Campaign for Nuclear Disarmament

Culture

Colin Wilson published; *Hancock's Half Hour* comedy series transfers from radio to television; Teddy Boys become visible; Elvis Presley releases 'Heartbreak Hotel'; American poet Allen Ginsberg publishes *Howl!*, a central Beat generation text; British artist Richard Hamilton's collage *What is it that makes today's homes so different, so appealing?* signals the beginning of pop art

The Entertainer by John Osborne first performed; *Declaration*, edited by Tom Maschler, published; Richard Hoggart's *The Uses of Literacy* published; David Lean's film *The Bridge on the River Kwai* released; *Daily Express* publishes homophobic articles about homosexuals; the Wolfenden Report recommends the decriminalization of homosexuality; Jack Kerouac publishes *On the Road*, a cult Beat novel; *The Uses of Literacy* by Richard Hoggart published

Epitaph for George Dillon by John Osborne and Anthony Creighton first performed; *The Birthday Party* by Harold Pinter first performed; *A Taste of Honey* by Shelagh Delaney first performed; *Saturday Night and Sunday Morning* by Alan Sillitoe published; first stereo gramophone

Politics	Culture
	records available in the United States; *Culture and Society* by Raymond Williams published; racist riots in London's Notting Hill
1959 The Conservatives win General Election, increasing their majority in Parliament	Film of *Look Back in Anger* released; *Room at the Top* film released; Billy Wilder's film *Some Like It Hot*, with Marilyn Monroe, released; *Roots* by Arnold Wesker first performed; *Kind of Blue* album by Miles Davies first released; Ronnie Scott's jazz club opens in London's Soho
1960 British Prime Minister Harold Macmillan makes the 'wind of change' speech about decolonization; Cyprus becomes independent; John F. Kennedy is elected 35th president of the United States	*The Caretaker* by Harold Pinter first performed; *Saturday Night and Sunday Morning* film released; *The Loneliness of the Long Distance Runner* by Alan Sillitoe published; Alfred Hitchcock's shocking film *Psycho* is released; oral contraceptive Pill is introduced in the United States; unexpurgated version of D. H. Lawrence's 1928 novel *Lady Chatterley's Lover* is published by Penguin Books after its prosecution for obscenity fails

Further Reading

The play

John Osborne, *Look Back in Anger*, London: Faber, 1957. The first edition of the play was published a year after its original opening and, although it was republished by Faber in 1960 and again in 1996, no significant changes have been made to the original text.

Two versions of the play are currently available on DVD: the 1958 film starring Richard Burton and Mary Ure, directed by Tony Richardson (MGM, 100 mins); the 1989 film starring Kenneth Branagh and Emma Thompson, directed by Judi Dench (Metrodome, 114 mins).

The playwright

Osborne, John, *A Better Class of Person*, London: Faber, 1981, and *Almost a Gentleman*, London, Faber, 1991. Reissued in one volume as *Looking Back: Never Explain, Never Apologise*, London: Faber, 1999. Two volumes of Osborne's autobiography, covering 1929–56 and 1955–66, are highly readable accounts of the playwright's life, full of anecdotes, aphorisms and quotes from his plays.

Osborne, John, *Damn You, England: Collected Prose*, London: Faber, 1994. Highly enjoyable collection of Osborne's provocative prose, from letters to articles and reviews, including 'A Letter to My Fellow Countrymen', 'They Call It Cricket' and his Obituary of George Devine.

Palmer, Tony, *John Osborne and the Gift of Friendship*, Five Arts, 2006. Excellent 128-minute DVD of a programme first broadcast on Channel 5 in 2006. Includes interviews with Osborne, Tony Richardson and David Hare, plus clips of classic performances by Laurence Olivier, Albert Finney and Nicol Williamson.

Heilpern, John, *John Osborne: A Patriot for Us*, London: Chatto & Windus, 2006. The official biography of Osborne, with detailed and fascinating material from his private diaries and papers. It includes a highly sympathetic account of the man and a passionate defence of the historical importance of *Look Back in Anger*.

The cultural context

Carpenter, Humphrey, *The Angry Young Men: A Literary Comedy of the 1950s*, London: Penguin, 2003. A readable and provocative account of the general cultural context of *Look Back in Anger* and the Angry Young Men, with interesting material about Kingsley Amis, Colin Wilson and John Braine, as well as Osborne.

Fowler, Jim, *Unleashing Britain: Theatre Gets Real 1955–64*, London: V&A, 2005. Released to coincide with the Theatre Museum's 2006 exhibition 'Unleashing Britain: Ten Years That Shaped the Nation 1955–64', this well-illustrated and simple account – which features pictures of the early productions of *Look Back in Anger* – places theatre in a wide cultural context.

Hewison, Robert, *In Anger: Culture in the Cold War 1945–60*, London: Methuen, 1988. The best and most engaging account of the general cultural context of *Look Back in Anger* and the Angry Young Men, with excellent material about Commitment and cultural politics in literature, cinema and television, as well as theatre.

Lacey, Stephen, *British Realist Theatre: The New Wave in Its Context 1956–1965*, London: Routledge, 1995. The most detailed and stimulating account of the economic, social, political and artistic context of the new wave in drama and cinema, with excellent accounts of *Look Back in Anger* as a play and as a film.

Rebellato, Dan, *1956 and All That: The Making of Modern British Drama*, London: Routledge, 1999. The best revisionist account of the historical importance of *Look Back in Anger*, with well-researched and fascinating insights into post-war British theatre culture and a rigorous command of post-structuralist theory.

Sandbrook, Dominic, *Never Had It So Good: A History of Britain from Suez to the Beatles*, London: Abacus, 2006. A readable and immensely detailed history of the late 1950s and early 1960s that covers culture as well as politics and economics in a clear and accessible way, providing a full historical context for *Look Back in Anger*.

Shellard, Dominic, *British Theatre Since the War*, New Haven: Yale University Press, 1999. The standard and stimulating account of the theatrical context of the new wave, with an excellent, well-researched and revisionist account of *Look Back in Anger* focusing on the role of critics such as Kenneth Tynan and the effects of theatre censorship.

Taylor, John Russell, *John Osborne: Look Back in Anger*, London: Macmillan Casebook, 1968. A very good selection of reviews and responses to the early productions of *Look Back in Anger*, with a handful of Osborne's own prose writings, and critical appraisals by Katherine J. Worth, George E. Wellwarth, John Mander and Mary McCarthy.

Wandor, Michelene, *Post-War British Drama: Looking Back in Gender*, London: Routledge, 2001. An updated version of her

1987 book, *Look Back in Gender*, this is a thought-provoking and convincingly argued feminist interpretation of the British New Wave plays of the 1950s and 1960s, and which now takes the story right up to the 1990s.

Wardle, Irving, *The Theatres of George Devine*, London: Jonathan Cape, 1978. The standard biography of George Devine explores the career and passions of the man who was Osborne's father figure. It explains the theatrical context of the 1950s, and the Royal Court's mission, with passionate clarity.

Websites

'Look Back in Anger', <http://en.wikipedia.org/wiki/Look_Back_in_Anger>. Solid entry about the 1956 play and the first film version from the online encyclopaedia.

'Look Back in Anger', <www.enotes.com/look-back/>. Enotes gives a summary and exam questions about the play.

Paul Bond, 'An inarticulate hope: Look Back in Anger by John Osborne', <www.wsws.org/articles/1999/sep1999/look-s14.shtml>. World Socialist offers a review of the 1999 National Theatre production and an account of the 1956 production.

Andrew Wyllie, 'Look Back in Anger', <www.litencyc.com/php/sworks.php?rec=true&UID=3921>. The Literary Encyclopedia gives an excellent overview of the play and its significance.

References

Note: All references to the play are to the 1996 reset edition: *Look Back in Anger*. London: Faber. References to Osborne's 'Foreword' (n. pag.) are to *Look Back in Anger*. London: Samuel French [undated: probably 1957], while his 'Introduction' is to Osborne, *Plays One: Look Back in Anger, Epitaph for George Dillon, The World of Paul Slickey, Déjà vu*. London: Faber. Osborne's 'They Call It Cricket' was published in Maschler, *Declaration* and 'That Awful Museum' reprinted in Taylor, *John Osborne: Look Back in Anger*.

All theatre programmes, and other documents related to specific stagings described in Chapter Three, can be found in production files held at the Theatre Museum Study Room, Blythe House, 23 Blythe Road, London W14 0QX. Website: <www.theatremuseum.org.uk>.

All references to interviews with the author are to the following:

Richard Baron, 4 October 2004.
Richard Coyle, 3 July 2006 and 29 September 2006.
Emma Fielding, 11 July 2006.
Peter Gill, 13 September 2005 and 12 June 2006.
Jacqueline Glasser, 21 September 2006.
David Hare, 10 September 2005.
Gregory Hersov, 14 February 2007.
Steve Hoggett and Scott Graham, 19 February 2004.
Marcus Romer, 1 March 2007.
Michael Sheen, 2 February 2007.
Derek Smith, 14 September 2006.
David Tennant, 20 October 2006.
Wendy Williams, 22 June 2006.

Allsop, Kenneth (1958), *The Angry Decade: A Survey of the Cultural Revolt of the Nineteen-Fifties*. London: Peter Owen.

Anderson, Lindsay (1957), 'Get out and push!', in Tom Maschler (ed.), *Declaration*. London: MacGibbon & Kee, pp. 153–78.

Anderson, Lindsay (1965), 'Vital theatre', in Charles Marowitz, Tom Milne and Owen Hale (eds), *The Encore Reader: A Chronicle of the New Drama*. London: Methuen, pp. 41–7.

Banham, Martin (1969), *Osborne*. Edinburgh: Oliver and Boyd.

Barthes, Roland (2000), *Mythologies* (trans. Annette Lavers). London: Vintage.

Billington, Michael (1999), 'The angry generation'. *Guardian*, 17 July.

Browne, Terry (1975), *Playwrights' Theatre: The English Stage Company at the Royal Court*. London: Pitman.

Bull, John (2004), 'The establishment of mainstream theatre, 1946–1979', in Baz Kershaw (ed.), *The Cambridge History of British Theatre*, Vol. 3: *Since 1895*. Cambridge: Cambridge University Press, pp. 326–48.

Burgess, Anthony (1984), *Ninety-Nine Novels: The Best in English Since 1939*. London: Alison & Busby.

Buse, Peter (2001), *Drama + Theory: Critical Approaches to Modern British Drama*. Manchester: Manchester University Press.

Coupland, Douglas (1992), *Generation X: Tales for an Accelerated Culture*. London: Abacus.

Coward, Noël (1999), *Collected Plays One: Hay Fever, The Vortex, Fallen Angels, Easy Virtue*. London: Methuen.

De Jongh, Nicholas (1992), *Not in Front of the Audience: Homosexuality on Stage*. London: Routledge.

De Jongh, Nicholas (2000), *Politics, Prudery and Perversions: The Censoring of the English Stage 1901–1968*. London: Methuen.

Edgar, David (1988), 'The diverse progeny of Jimmy Porter', in his *The Second Time as Farce: Reflections on the Drama of Mean Times*. London: Lawrence and Wishart, pp. 137–42.

Edgar, David (ed.) (1999), *State of Play: Playwrights on Playwriting*. London: Faber.

Eliot, T. S. (1960), *The Waste Land and Other Poems*. London: Faber.

Foucault, Michel (1976), *The History of Sexuality Volume 1: An Introduction* (trans. Robert Hurley). London: Allen Lane.

Fowler, Jim (2005), *Unleashing Britain: Theatre Gets Real 1955–64*. London: V&A.

Gibbons, Fiachra (1999), 'Angry Young Men under fire from gay writer'. *Guardian*, 8 November.

Gill, A. A. (2005), *The Angry Island: Hunting the English*. London: Weidenfeld & Nicolson.

Gilleman, Luc (2002), *John Osborne: Vituperative Artist*. New York: Routledge.

Griffiths, Gareth (1981), *John Osborne: Look Back in Anger*. Harlow, Essex: Longman.

Hall, Stuart (1965a), 'Something to live for', in Charles Marowitz, Tom Milne and Owen Hale (eds), *The Encore Reader: A Chronicle of the New Drama*. London: Methuen, pp. 110–15.

Hall, Stuart (1965b), 'Beyond naturalism pure', in Charles Marowitz, Tom Milne and Owen Hale (eds), *The Encore Reader: A Chronicle of the New Drama*. London: Methuen, pp. 212–20.

Hare, David (2005), *Obedience, Struggle & Revolt: Lectures on Theatre*. London: Faber.

Hayman, Ronald (1969), *John Osborne* (2nd edn). London: Heinemann Contemporary Playwrights.

Heilpern, John (2006), *John Osborne: A Patriot for Us*, London: Chatto & Windus.

Hewison, Robert (1988), *In Anger: Culture in the Cold War 1945–60*. London: Methuen.

Hill, John (1986), *Sex, Class and Realism: British Cinema 1956–1963*. London: British Film Institute.

Hobson, Harold (1984), *Theatre in Britain: A Personal View*. Oxford: Phaidon.

Innes, Christopher (1992), *Modern British Drama 1890–1990*. Cambridge: Cambridge University Press.

Lacey, Stephen (1995), *British Realist Theatre: The New Wave in Its Context 1956–1965*. London: Routledge.

Lacey, Stephen (2006), 'The moment of *Look Back in Anger* and post-war cultural history'. Paper given at the '1956, 1968, 1979, 1995: New Historiographies of Post-War British Theatre' conference at Royal Holloway, University of London, 11–13 May.

Lawson, Mark (2006), 'Fifty years of anger'. *Guardian*, 31 March.

Leavis, F. R. (1962), *The Great Tradition*. Harmondsworth: Penguin.

Luckhurst, Mary (2006), '1956 and the centrality of misogyny'. Paper given at the '1956, 1968, 1979, 1995: New Historiographies of Post-War British Theatre' conference at Royal Holloway, University of London, 11–13 May.

McCarthy, Mary (1968), 'A new word', in John Russell Taylor (ed.), *John Osborne: Look Back in Anger*. London: Macmillan Casebook, pp. 150–60.

Mander, John (1968), 'The writer and commitment', in John Russell Taylor (ed.), *John Osborne: Look Back in Anger*. London: Macmillan Casebook, pp. 143–9.

Marowitz, Charles, Tom Milne and Owen Hale (eds) (1965), *The Encore Reader: A Chronicle of the New Drama*. London: Methuen.

Maschler, Tom (ed.) (1957), *Declaration*. London: MacGibbon & Kee.

Osborne, John [1957], *Look Back in Anger*. London: Samuel French.

Osborne, John (1961), *The Entertainer*. London: Faber.

Osborne, John (1981), *A Better Class of Person*. London: Faber.

Osborne, John (1991), *Almost a Gentleman*. London, Faber.

Osborne, John (1994), *Damn You, England: Collected Prose*. London: Faber.

Osborne, John (1996a), *Look Back in Anger*. London: Faber.

Osborne, John (1996b), *Plays One: Look Back in Anger, Epitaph for George Dillon, The World of Paul Slickey, Déjà vu*. London: Faber.

Palmer, Tony (2006), *John Osborne and the Gift of Friendship*. DVD, Five Arts.

Priestley, J. B. (1969), *Time and the Conways and Other Plays*. Harmondsworth: Penguin.

Rebellato, Dan (1999), *1956 and All That: The Making of Modern British Drama*. London: Routledge.

Rebellato, Dan (2006), 'Looking back at anger', in *Contemporary Theatre Review*. Vol. 16, Issue 4 (November): 527–9.

Richardson, Tony (1993), *Long Distance Runner: A Memoir*. London: Faber.

Ritchie, Harry (1988), *Success Stories: Literature and the Media in England, 1950–1959*. London: Faber.

Roberts, Philip (1999), *The Royal Court Theatre and the Modern Stage*. Cambridge: Cambridge University Press.

Sandbrook, Dominic (2006), *Never Had It So Good: A History of Britain from Suez to the Beatles*. London: Abacus.

Shellard, Dominic (1999), *British Theatre Since the War*. New Haven: Yale University Press.

Shuttleworth, Ian (1995), *Ken & Em: The Biography of Kenneth Branagh and Emma Thompson*. London: Headline.

Sierz, Aleks (1996), 'John Osborne and the myth of anger', in *New Theatre Quarterly*, No. 46 (May): 136–46.

Sinfield, Alan (1989), *Literature, Politics and Culture in Post-war Britain*. Oxford: Blackwell.

Situationist International, *Internationale Situationniste 1953–69* (Reprint). Champs Libre, Paris, 1975.

Taylor, John Russell (ed.) (1968), *John Osborne: Look Back in Anger – A Casebook*. London: Macmillan.

Taylor, John Russell (1969), *Anger and After: A Guide to the New British Drama* (rev. edn). London: Eyre Methuen.

Theatre Museum (2006), 'Unleashing Britain: ten years that shaped the nation 1955–64'. Theatre Museum exhibition, London.

Trussler, Simon (1969), *The Plays of John Osborne: An Assessment*. London: Victor Gollancz.

Tynan, Kenneth (2007), *Theatre Writings* (ed. Dominic Shellard). London: Nick Hern.

Walker, Alexander (1974), *Hollywood England: The British Film Industry in the Sixties*. London: Michael Joseph.

Wandor, Michelene (2001), *Post-War British Drama: Looking Back in Gender*. London: Routledge.

Wardle, Irving (1978), *The Theatres of George Devine*. London: Jonathan Cape.

Watt, David (1965), 'Class report', in Charles Marowitz, Tom Milne and Owen Hale (eds), *The Encore Reader: A Chronicle of the New Drama*. London: Methuen, pp. 56–62.

Whitebrook, Peter (2005), 'Look Back in Anger'. Programme note to the Lyceum Theatre, Edinburgh, production of the play, January.

Worth, Katherine J. (1968), 'The Angry Young Man', in John Russell Taylor (ed.), *John Osborne: Look Back in Anger*. London: Macmillan Casebook, pp. 101–16.

Index